It's not often one gets to read a novel that moves one to tears and laughter in what could otherwise have been a laborious case study. *Outbound Air* reads as a docudrama with a powerful storyline. Anyone from the corporate world, especially dealing with venture capital, will have experienced or administered much of the pain, suffering, and sorrow when the bottom line is taken care of at the expense of the top line. All organizations are about people.

Outbound Air puts flesh, bone along with emotion into what can go wrong when profit relegates values to words on a wall and disregards the profitability of morality. No single snowflake takes responsibility for the avalanche. Yet the success of a high performance organization is based on each individual taking responsibility and total accountability for the success of the enterprise by doing their work competently with total commitment.

Such powerful teaching moments easily remembered because one remembers the story. Tom Foster reminds us of what Emerson shared in his Journals (of 1836) about what is the hardest task in the world – To THINK.

Welcome home. You are about to begin the most important read of your day.

– *Austin "Ozzie" Gontang, Ph.D. Vistage Chair, San Diego, CA*

Tom Foster is an expert in the practical implementation of the research and management science of Dr. Elliott Jaques. Jaques strategies provide a logical foundation for the construction of a complex yet viable company structure. In today's globalized world, these lessons are necessary for effective and efficient business operations. – *Dr. William Kent, CEO, Horner Express*

Tom Foster has been deftly teaching the lessons of Elliot Jaques for years. His book *Hiring Talent*, about interviewing and hiring to appropriate *levels of work*, has been used in our fast growth technology company with great success. It helped our hiring managers understand what it *means* to be a hiring manager. In his new book, *Outbound Air*, Foster uses his story telling style to teach *levels of work* throughout each phase in a company's growth. *Outbound Air* teaches important lessons about *levels of work* in organizational structure to managers at every level. – *James Cline, CFO, United Data Technologies*

Tom's book is a wonderful way to learn about time span and how Elliott Jaques' crucial discovery plays out in action. This easy to read story provides a template for pulling a dysfunctional executive team together through clarity and purpose rather than rope-climbing and scavenger hunts. In doing this, you are effortlessly worked through a sound way to create clear organisational structure at the functional level through the collective contribution of all. But don't read this only for the important knowledge, read this to enjoy a great business story. – *Adam Thompson, Partner, The Working Journey, Head Office Australia*

The author of this book is a friend of mine. When I started reading *Outbound Air*, I thought he was writing about me and my former company. So many details were the same. Owner entrepreneurs' sale of their babies is very typical of the company in this book. When a small company grows, understanding time span is critical for the growth of the company. I would like to thank Tom for making *levels of work* easy to understand. This is a great read for aspiring managers. – *Tim O'Connor, former owner, Town and Country Industries*

Tom Foster had an incredible impact on my approach to "putting the right people on the bus" in every aspect of my company by defining job roles, the level of work and time span of that work. He creates the right questions of candidates for those positions to understand their capability related to the work in their current role and capability in future roles. This book is a narrative of that process and essential reading for anyone in business. I have used Tom's techniques and the research of Elliot Jaques to successfully move my business from one that was family run on "tribal knowledge" to one that is run by a qualified team with strong systems and procedures. *Outbound Air* prints the roadmap for future growth. Thanks Tom! – *Michael Grimme, CEO, AMC Liquidators*

Tom Foster skillfully applies the research of Dr. Elliot Jaques to this fictional account of a small airline recently sold to a capital investment firm. The story weaves many real life experiences from Tom's years of working with business owners as a Chair to several Vistage (formerly TEC) Groups into the tale. In particular, the experience of the owner post-sale is a warning to all those considering selling their business. My favorite part is when the woman CEO reorganizes the company and brings about strategic change (using the concepts taught by Elliott Jaques) that saves the company in spite of some selfish motives of those who would derail her plans. Her courage under fire is a tribute to women in business. – *Catherine Colan Muth, CEO, O. R. Colan Group, LLC*

"This book brings the reality of truth into perspective. Through the narrative, Tom demonstrates not only the pragmatics of Elliot Jaques and other thought leaders in both the understanding, as well as, the broadly applicable example of the "how" it works in practice, day-to-day." – Dick Shorten, Chairman, Vistage NJ

Outbound Air

Levels of Work in
Organizational Structure

Thank you for your interest in the Research of Elliott Jaques.

~Tom Foster

Outbound Air
Levels of Work in Organizational Structure

Dedication

Outbound Air is dedicated to the memory of Blake Bennett. Blake listened. He learned. To the end, he was a curious student of Elliott's research and a disciplined practitioner.

Acknowledgments

There are many people who inspired and helped with this project. In 2000, Jerry Harvey (*The Abilene Paradox*, and *How Come Every Time I Get Stabbed in the Back, My Fingerprints Are On the Knife*) introduced me to the research of Dr. Elliott Jaques. He recommended a short book written by Elliott, which thoroughly confused me. Three months later, I finally made heads and tails of its implications and that began an odyssey.

Elliott Jaques passed away March 8, 2003. I had just finished reading *Social Power and the CEO* (2002), and embarked on *The Life and Behavior of Living Organisms* (2002), when I heard the news from Glenn Waring.

By then, I was hooked. I spent a year attempting to describe Elliott's research to many of my clients. Rick Oppenheimer found out what I was doing and, in 2004 invited me to talk to his executive peer groups in Lancaster, Pennsylvania. Rick described his group's experience in an internet chat room and that put me solidly on the road.

A couple of years passed before I met with Kathryn Cason, Elliott's widow. She was easily 50 percent of the intellectual property of Elliott's research in the later years of his life. I spent eight grueling hours as she reviewed and critiqued my presentation materials. She made 65 changes to the PowerPoint visuals. All for the better. "It's not that complicated," she said, explaining the elegant simplicity at the heart of the research.

I want to thank Mitch Talenfeld, Tim O'Connor, Dan Kaiserian and Mike Grimme for leaping with both feet into the original manuscript and coaching me through its initial drafts.

James Cline guided me through the financial storyline. Bob Plath lent me his airline eyes as a pilot. Rick Reposa assisted in the operational flight sequences. My hat is off to everyone who helped my understanding over the past couple of decades.

Table of Contents

Why read this book

Every management team wants to take their company to the next level. Most have no clue what that means. I press for answers and get general responses, like –

- Higher revenues
- Larger geography
- More stores

I am a structure guy, and levels actually exist. Each level in the life of a company has defined characteristics and carries predictable challenges that must be solved before the organization can go to the next level. This book answers the question that no one asks, "Just exactly what *is* the next level?"

These levels teach us about organizational structure. This structure helps a company understand why it has its problems and how to solve them. This book is about the structure of work, specifically –

- Predictable levels of organizational growth, a prelude to *levels of work*.

- *Levels of work* and accountability, in both managerial relationships and cross-functional relationships.

- How to implement functional structure based on *levels of work*.

The safety briefing is over, buckle up and prepare for an immediate departure.

–Tom Foster

Part One

Ink on the Contract

The ink on the contract was dry. Jim Dunbar had mixed emotions, somewhere between joy and happiness. With lingering pangs of seller's remorse, he felt, in the end, he made the right decision to sell his company, Outbound Air.

His cellphone vibrated a gentle chirp. Everything Jim worked for, during the better part of three decades, was about to go sideways. On the phone was Keith Sutton, Jim's right hand man, now, former right hand man. In spite of a guaranteed employment contract during the transition to the new owner, Keith was just terminated.

"It was humiliating," Keith explained. "I thought we were on a guaranteed six month contract after you sold the company. You said the management team was going to remain intact, at least for the time being. The new CEO didn't waste much time. It took him less than a week to fire us all. He even had security pack our stuff and escort us out of the building."

Jim's next call was to his attorney, Henry Barrat.

"We negotiated an airtight contract," Jim stammered. "Henry, it took us two weeks to iron out the details of that one single provision in the agreement. I thought the whole deal was dead because I wanted security for my best managers in the sale. In the end, they finally agreed and promised six months employment. In six months, I knew my executive team could prove their value. It's been less than a week and the new CEO is already handing out pink slips."

"I know," Henry replied. "As soon as we hang up I will put a call into Fran Smith. I negotiated across the table with her for several hours. Even though she works for the other side, I am sure her understanding was the same as yours. My guess is, she is aware of these terminations, too. Let me call her."

"Never mind," Jim said. "I called you because I needed to let off a little steam. I will call her. This new CEO, Ripley, must have made a mistake. Maybe, he didn't read the contract. It's going to be a tough pill for him to swallow, having to take back his first announcement. Let's keep you out of it for the moment. I don't want everyone upset, hearing from an attorney before we have things sorted out. Once Ripley reads the contract, I am sure he will backtrack and smooth things over."

Jim touched the number next to the name Fran Smith on his cellphone. He met Fran ten months earlier. She headed the acquisition team for Coriolis, the holding company that bought Jim's company.

"I was expecting your call," Fran said. "I got the news five minutes ago. I can't believe what I heard. This was not what we negotiated with you."

"Fran, you know I am a reasonable guy," Jim started. "I am sure it was a mistake. This fellow, Ripley, probably wanted to bring in his own team and didn't read the contract. I can't believe he wasn't briefed. This is going to be embarrassing for him. I mean, Coriolis has owned my company for a week and he has only been on the ground for two days."

"Let me call him," Fran replied. "It will be better if he hears this from me. It will be delicate, but I am sure we can straighten this out."

"Fran, just to make sure, why don't you set up a meeting for me? I need to meet Ripley sooner or later. Sooner would be better."

"Will do. Listen, Jim. I am actually in St. Louis right now, working on another acquisition, so you will have to take this meeting on your own."

"I can handle that," Jim assured her.

Dry Run

Jim sat in the open area, outside what used to be his own office, waiting for Al Ripley. It seemed odd, to be in a place where his role, now, shifted so dramatically. The new gatekeeper at the desk, politely served him coffee, as a guest. Not in a company mug, but in a small Styrofoam cup.

"Mr. Ripley has you on the calendar," she confirmed. "And I worked for him at another company. He is always punctual, a very intentional man."

Jim Dunbar was also punctual, but this morning he was early. Ten minutes to the appointed time. He stood up to shake off his pent-up energy. It was twenty four hours since that first phone call and he was anxious to get some resolution to this predicament. Damage control was going to be bad enough, but the more time that elapsed, the more difficult the fix.

Five minutes to the appointed time. Jim found himself looking at the new teamwork posters on the wall. Fifty people jumping out of an airplane holding hands. It was an attractive poster, he had seen it a hundred times featured in airline magazines. Jim wondered why it never occurred to him to buy something like that. Nice touch from the new guy, he thought.

Time ticked by, a quarter past. Jim's face did not move as he lifted his eyes to the guardian behind the desk. She worked for Al Ripley long enough to know the script. "I am so sorry. I just got an email from Mr. Ripley. He was detained in a conference call with Mr. Pierce. He is the Chairman of the Board. One time zone to the east, you know how it is. Mr. Ripley took the call from his home this morning. He stopped the call long enough to let me know. Would it be convenient to schedule another time."

Jim stood up, "But this meeting is terribly important."

"I know," said the gatekeeper. "Mr. Ripley planned to explain why the executive terminations were necessary."

"But I don't think he understands," Jim furrowed his brow.

"Yes, he understands," she replied politely. "He told me you would be calling. Mr. Ripley is a man of integrity. He said the company would stand behind the severance packages you negotiated, each member of the executive team would be paid in full."

Jim felt the temperature rise along his shoulders. The messenger behind the desk was wrong. Jim wanted to set things straight, but realized he was speaking with the wrong person. "I apologize," he said. "Perhaps we can schedule another time with Mr. Ripley."

Stepping into the hallway, Jim realized how alone he was. Ripley left him to twist in the wind. Keith Sutton, by now, must realize that all the promises Jim made to the executive team were empty. He checked his phone for messages, not a text or an email from anyone, not even his attorney. At first, Jim was in denial, certain this whole thing was a mistake, but the truth began to settle. He wanted to fight it, renegotiate something that was already negotiated, but there was no one on the other side of the table.

Alone, he stood in the hallway, empty of chatter, silent. Jim Dunbar was supposed to be on top of the world. He could only imagine how Keith Sutton explained to his family, how he was fired. Jim promised the team that the sale of the company would be good for everyone. "Coriolis has resources to invest in new ground equipment, new planes," he said. "Their employee benefit package is an upgrade." Everything Jim promised was a ruse. And he was to blame. His status moved from hero to goat in the space of a few days.

Jim felt a vibration on his belt. He reached for the plastic holster and slid the glass screen forward. It was an email from Fran. With a swipe of a finger, the screen display collapsed and swirled a message that Fran had not the courage to deliver, nor even the will to translate. It was a forwarded text from Al Ripley. Fran's message at the top, simply said, "I'm sorry, Jim."

"Fran, I don't know why you are upset," the message began. "You know the six month severance package is standard in all of our takeover deals. It is clearly spelled out in the contract with Dunbar. Too bad if his attorney couldn't read and understand it. If he had better counsel, he would have fought for some real concessions. Not my concern now. I called a meeting with the new management team for next week. When you talk to Jim, tell him, 'no hard feelings.' And just to prove it, tell him he is invited to the management meeting, too. In fact, there are some things I need to discuss about his earn-out. Jim left most of his money on the table, let's make him work for it. –Al Ripley."

Jim let his head drop. He pressed a button and the screen display raced to a bright white pinpoint, then disappeared. Walking in a daze, Jim looked up to find himself on the sidewalk outside his office building. Jim never kicked in a door or fist-punched a hole in a sheetrock wall. He never kicked a dog in his path or shouted obscenities at a passing car. But Jim was angry.

Phone in hand, he touched a familiar picture on the speed dial. Henry Barrat had been Jim's corporate attorney for the better part of 25 years.

"What the hell, Henry? Did we really get hoodwinked?" Jim asked. "I re-read the agreement about the employment period for my executive team. It is very specific about the salary guarantee and its duration. It never occurred to me that Ripley intended to pay it out as severance, with no commitment to retain the team."

"I am afraid so, Jim," Henry replied. "But I have more news. I just received a certified letter from that Ripley character. At first, I thought it was a letter of congratulations, but it came certified. The letter simply restates the language in the acquisition agreement about your consulting contract. You know we negotiated most of the goodwill in the purchase price to a consulting agreement. Ripley expects you to report for work next week, says he expects a full forty hours from you."

"But that consulting agreement was just a formality," Jim protested. "We structured that just to spread the purchase price into three tax years and create deductibility for the company. I mean, I expected to help out a bit during the transition, so I am not sure what he has up his sleeve."

"I don't know either," Henry replied. "I will email you a copy of this letter. You can decide. Could be, he is just flexing his muscle, maybe he will relax after a couple of weeks. You should be able to get a read on him pretty quick."

"I'm afraid I already have a good read on him," Jim replied.

Most Important Work

Jim's car rolled into the driveway. He touched a button to open the garage door. He sat in the car, waiting for the rolling aluminum to stop in its track. Above the passage into the house, his attention went to a familiar sign tacked above the door. "Welcome home, Jim. You are about to begin the most important work of your day."

There was a point in Jim's career when he almost forgot about home, his family, his refuge from the world. It was a high point, when things at Outbound Air moved fast. Exciting. Working twelve hour days, Jim arrived home one evening, drenched in exuberant exhaustion. His two kids were at friends, his wife gone shopping. Nothing was wrong except the quiet of the house. Jim never believed in work-life balance. His work was his life and his life was his work. But the quiet disturbed him, even his dog was asleep in the corner of the living room.

Jim thought to himself, that day, "I work really hard, and I like hard work. But if I lose this, if I lose this family, this quiet place, what is the point?" He went to the garage, found a discarded piece of wood, an old paint can and brush. As carefully as he could, with free hand, he painted a solid background and the words to remind him.

Jim snapped back to reality, the garage swallowed his car into its womb. The engine went silent and he walked through the door, underneath the sign to begin the most important work of his day.

His wife, Susan looked up from her iPad, propped up on the kitchen counter. She liked her technology, but could never sit still for long. After medical school, Susan migrated to North Dakota to start her own practice. She met Jim, 25 years ago, when he reported for a mandatory physical to qualify for his pilot's license.

Susan didn't speak. She didn't have to. Jim locked eye contact and moved across the room. The iPad was dark when they separated their embrace.

Jim tried to make sense of his day, out loud. Susan could hear the unspoken anger in his voice, but only quietly listened. He was not complaining, but trying to piece together the logic underneath the sequence of events. Most importantly, he was trying to imagine what would unfold the following week. As they talked, the sun slipped behind a cloud and disappeared beyond the horizon. A scarlet parade of haze shimmered before a sudden darkness.

The Cave

Jim woke up early the next morning and stole away into his study. He often worked from home, in this room, outfitted with a flat panel TV, two ceiling height bookshelves, lots of table surface and a well-worn chair. As he sat in the dark, the morning light glowed through the windows. Jim stood and dropped the shades. The flat screen stayed dark. He needed quiet to think. He needed to shut out the world, with all its distractions. On the desk, in the dark, sat the contract. But it was only there for its object. The words, reviewed so many times that Jim committed them to memory, along with all the red lines and negotiating points. How had he been so stupid? How did he not see the ambiguity in the legal sentences so artfully crafted?

Susan slowly pushed open the door. It was full morning in the rest of the house. She carried a cup of coffee, steam rising through its milk froth. Jim smiled a genuine response, but did not speak. Susan smiled a knowing acknowledgement that Jim was in his cave. He shut off the rest of the world, blocked out all its stimuli. Left to his own thoughts, Jim watched Susan back out of the room and silently close the door.

Jim was always a planner, but this scenario stumped him. After the sale, he looked forward to a short break from the responsibilities of running his company. The deflation after the closing was a welcome state. In the back of his mind, he planned to steal Susan away for a couple of weeks. But here he was, aware. He saw what happened, but did not know why. Less than a week clicked by and he was back in the thick of things, on high alert.

Two days in the cave, unshaven, with only sparse amounts of food, Jim gathered himself on Monday morning. The warm shaving cream hit his face, but the razor tugged at two days growth. It was his turn to make the coffee as he poured the hot water over the grounds and watched the drip through the filter.

"Are you back?" Susan said, lining up her coffee mug behind his.

Jim nodded his head and smiled. "Yes, I'm back. Just needed to think."

"Did you figure it out?" she asked.

"Nope. Nothing has really changed. Except, it is, what it is. I know where I stand. I am not happy about it, but I am clear in my head. There is the transition meeting this morning. I'm ready for it. I have my feet on the ground. Let's go see what Mr. Ripley has in store for me, today."

"You were pretty dark over the weekend," Susan observed.

"Yes, I agree."

Late

Jim arrived ten minutes early for the meeting. He resolved to keep an open mind. Though he had privileged knowledge of Ripley's email to Fran, Jim believed it was better to stay on the high road.

Outside the conference room, he thought it odd there was no mingling. He hoped to meet some of the new players, introduce himself. After all, he was the former CEO, he could at least welcome the new team. He pushed open the door and instantly became the center of attention. At the head of the table sat Al Ripley. On either side were minions of suits. Jim could smell the starch of white shirts in the room. Crisp, striped neckties reinforced the odor of formality.

"You're late," Ripley said.

It was understood that Jim's employment agreement was necessary to support the compensation earn-out, but it was also understood that, after the initial transition, Jim's actual time commitment would be minimal for the three year payout period. Jim was assigned a sparse desk and chair, but, it was a gentlemen's understanding that he would rarely, if ever, sit at that desk. Until today.

"I'm sorry," Jim apologized.

"Take a seat, we already started," Ripley commanded.

Al Ripley talked a good game. In this first transition meeting, he spoke about vision, mission and culture. He ordered teamwork posters to be mounted all around the complex. This was not Al Ripley's first rodeo. His words were politically correct, but empty.

Three minutes elapsed between Jim's entrance and the end of the meeting. "All right, you guys know what to do. Let's whip this airline into shape," Ripley concluded. "Dunbar. I will see you in my office. Ten minutes."

Man to Man

"I am sorry I was late to the meeting," Jim started. "The email I got, said 9:00am."

"We changed the meeting time," Ripley interrupted. "You should have double-checked. Look, Dunbar, I will get right to the point. I know this company was your baby, but it is now a wholly owned subsidiary of Coriolis. We have big plans for this little airline.

"And I know your purchase contract outlines a three year earn-out based on operating profit from paid passenger revenue. Your attorney may not have clearly understood that you actually have to work for that earn-out.

"You were assigned a desk in the bull pen, but I changed that. I let Keith Sutton go, so you can have his office. Nice corner window.

"You know, Jim," Ripley shifted from last name to first name. "Teamwork and culture are critically important for any company. And that's your job. Your longevity with this airline will be based on company morale. Chief Culture Officer, that's your new title.

25

Now, I am going to drive people pretty hard. It will be up to you to pump up the troops and keep them motivated.

"And, Jim," Ripley continued. "Don't think this will be a walk in the park. If you expect this company to honor its agreement on your payout, you are going to have to earn it."

As Jim walked toward Keith Sutton's old office, he was calm. He did not take the conversation personally. Jim knew people like Ripley. Approaching the door, he noticed Keith Sutton's name plate was missing, replaced with one bearing his own name, subtitled – Chief Culture Officer. It seemed odd. The name plate matched a new set of business cards on the desk, Keith Sutton's telephone extension behind the phone number. This transition had Jim off balance, but it apparently was planned in some detail, weeks in advance.

Part Two

Before the Acquisition

Eleven months before the acquisition, Jim's cellphone vibrated. It was not a number in his directory, but he answered anyway. The voice on the other end belonged to Fran Smith, who said she was a business broker.

"I have a group of investors interested in buying companies like yours. We watched your operation at Outbound Air for the last year and want to know if I might come down to take a closer look."

Jim received calls like this from time to time. The discussions never went anywhere. The inquiry was usually an investment group on a fishing expedition, bottom feeders.

The thought of selling Outbound occasionally pushed to the surface of Jim's mind. At 60 years old, he felt young, but no longer invincible. His sense of independence kept him in denial that his company, someday, might grow beyond him or that he might reach his personal limits of leadership. At times, he wondered if Outbound Air might require a higher level of organization and structure.

His sense of responsibility to his management team was high. What would happen if he abandoned ship? What if the new captain was a tyrant, without a sense of history or connection to the people who committed their best years to Outbound?

But this inquiry seemed different. Maybe it was time. At the end of the phone call, they settled on the following Thursday, at a quiet restaurant in Denver.

Face to Face

That Thursday morning found Jim Dunbar in the air. Though he rarely flew a scheduled leg, he kept up his pilot rating. Today, he was co-pilot bound for Denver. Sitting in the right seat of the cockpit, his mood turned nostalgic. His love of flying, his passion for building this small regional airline might come to an end. What would life be like after building and selling Outbound Air?

Pushing through the door of the restaurant, Jim Dunbar met Fran Smith. "I saw your picture on the website," she explained.

Self-described as a portfolio manager, Fran worked for a small group of investors as a hired gun. Over the next few hours, if the conversation went anywhere, it would be her decision from the investor side and Jim's decision from his side.

Fran appeared young, but spoke with the clout of experience. She grew up in a small family business that her parents sold during her college years. Most of the proceeds went for their retirement, but her parents carved out a small financial stake to help Fran start her first business out of school, a photocopy service right off campus. She built up her small enterprise to five machines and twenty employees in less than three months' time.

One year out of college and one year into business, Fran fell in love with a graduate student from out of state. When the love of her life proposed marriage, the caveat required a move away from the city where Fran grew up, away from her small business which, now, had three locations.

Fran described the inflection point that changed her life forever. Her parents were in a position to give her counsel on how to sell her business. It seems, she was not the only one, at the time, who saw the market potential for photocopy centers near a college campus.

The good news, she did well on the sales transaction, and free from the tether of her own business, followed the love of her life back to his home town. The bad news, he was better at graduate school than finding a job. Outside of a liberal arts environment, the realities of the world of work broke their relationship.

Two important things happened to Fran during this time. She got a taste for starting and selling a business and her life was still packed in a storage trailer. Twenty-eight years later, she traveled the country buying and selling companies for Coriolis.

And on this late afternoon, across the table, sat Jim Dunbar. Enough of the chit-chat. She wanted to know more about Jim, his business and its role in the market. She had a company to buy and if it was not Jim's company, she had another on her list.

"We both signed non-disclosure agreements," she started, "so I want the whole story. We will get to due-diligence later, but I need to know who you are. Tell me how you got started, why you got started. And don't sugarcoat things. If you tell me that your airline was the result of a perfect strategic plan, flawlessly executed, I will know you are lying. So, the good, the bad and the ugly."

And, then Fran stopped. And she waited. Jim finally spoke.

Level I

"In the beginning, it was me," Jim started. "I had this hare-brained notion about flying for an airline. As a kid, I was a member of the Civil Air Patrol. It started out as a hobby, maybe should have stayed a hobby. You could say I had a cause, but it's more like the cause had me. I started the company because I had an idea that I thought might work."

Fran moved her water glass to the side, to focus her attention on the story Jim was about to tell.

"I flew back and forth, from my home in Dickinson, North Dakota to Denver. My passengers were a couple of buddies of mine, in the oil business. I got the flying hours. My friends would pay for fuel and the operating

29

reserve on the airplane. My weekly trips turned into twice a week, then three times a week.

"A big oil shale project ramped up in North Dakota, so pretty soon, we saw pickup trucks with Halliburton signs on the side. Every motel in town was booked solid. That's when things turned over. I was no longer flying just my friends, now I was flying strangers.

"I had to step up my level of service, brought catering on board. I began to run a schedule and take reservations. Moving from a charter operation to scheduled service meant we had more compliance issues. Safety compliance was our biggest concern. Those airlines that talk about friendly skies and tout customer service are fooling themselves. What airlines do really well is cram dozens of people into a big metal tube, hurl it through the air at three, four hundred miles an hour and land that metal tube without killing anybody. Everything else is fluff.

"We were a start-up, and start-ups seldom make money in the beginning. Our banker was supportive. He knew, for the time being, we lived on our line of credit. But we showed promise.

"I collected a few friends around me, people I knew, that were either between jobs, had a crappy job or just plain bored. We were a happy group. We worked hard all week, ten, twelve hours a day. Every Friday, we brought in a case of beer and a tub of potato chips to celebrate our little airline.

"We didn't have a marketing department, the web was barely invented. We put up a schedule on the bulletin board in the terminal building in Dickinson. That was it. It was all about flying.

"I guess it was predictable, we had negative cash flow," Jim explained. "There is a high level of risk in every start-up, most fail in the first five years. So, it seemed normal that we struggled.

"But those were the good old days. Funny, when I think back, we didn't have many management issues, but then, there weren't that many people to manage."

		Organizational Growth[i]			
Level	Time Span Outlook	Organizational Characteristics	Organizational Challenge	Management Challenge	Necessary Focus
I	1d-3m	High risk of sustainability	Negative cash flow	Little or no management depth	Make sales. Introduce product or service into the market. Find a customer, any customer, to buy.

Fran leaned forward. This was what she wanted to hear. She wanted to understand the struggles, how they made decisions and solved problems.

Level II

"We survived, in part, through sheer determination and blind dumb luck. But we never gave up. And as time went by, we got more passengers. Our first schedules flew because it was convenient for me. I mean, I was the pilot.

"At the time we didn't own our plane. We had a pretty sweet lease arrangement, but a couple of things happened. We flew so often, I moved from the only pilot, to the lead pilot, to an occasional right-side pilot. We found so many people wanted to fly with us that we needed another plane. But the lease deal on the second plane wasn't as sweet as the first plane. Truth be told, we couldn't afford the second lease. We tried to fill in with the odd aircraft, but when you run scheduled service, you have to have dedicated equipment.

"That which does not kill you, makes you stronger," Jim grinned. "Our momentum told us we were not likely to die, at least not in that fiscal year. We were invincible. So, I signed a lease on the second plane.

"Passenger loads picked up, and I had to hire more people. And that led to a predictable stumble. There was no rhyme or reason for the way we did things. We survived on our tenacity, but our tenacity began to fail us. My wife described our behavior as improvisation. Invincibility and improvisation make for a toxic cocktail. We over-promised, extended our thin resources.

"I remember our first overbooking. We had more passengers than seats. I looked at my schedule, figured we could make the run to Denver, flip the aircraft around and come back for the other group. For some reason, we thought the stranded passengers would wait the four hours. But, a weather system moved in. In spite of our promises, we never made it back, and missed another flight leg with a scheduled full plane.

"The second plane increased our capacity and allowed us to look at additional cities. We hired more people, but that brought its own chaos as things became more complicated. Now, we had management issues. We were our own worst enemy.

"We were constantly late. At first, our customers just grumbled a bit, but then, the unthinkable happened. We had a formal customer complaint. The customer wrote me a personal letter and sent a copy to the local paper. Now, nobody reads the weekly newspaper in Dickinson, but a reporter in Kansas City, Harry Richter, picked it up and created some embarrassing press. Something had to change.

"To say we flew by the seat of our pants was an understatement. But, at the time, I figured that my team had practiced for months, we successfully flew one plane, how difficult could it be with two planes?

"I am not a math whiz, but even I could figure it out. After the newspaper article, 50 percent of our seats flew empty. I couldn't apologize to passengers that weren't there anymore."

Fran's face remained curious, so Jim kept talking.

"It was not a matter of catching our schedule problems and fixing them. It was a matter of preventing schedule problems in the first place.

"In the beginning, everyone did a little bit of everything and that approach served us well, but, now, it had to go," Jim pursed his lips. "We had to stop. As an organization, we had to regroup and think about the work. It was painful to slow down. We canceled some flights and grounded our second aircraft to create the short space we needed to organize.

"We had to define and document our methods and processes. We had to identify the way we positioned aircraft, how we put together flight schedules and how many people we needed to do each thing. As we defined the steps in each process, it came naturally, to divide those steps and assign different people to different roles. We had specialized players, who got really good at each assigned task. They documented the best way to achieve each step and they practiced. They practiced to mastery."

Fran detected a bit of pride in Jim's description.

"The company now had a group of master operators, individually focused on each step in the process, but we still had a problem. While each step was masterfully done, sometimes, there were gaps between steps, and sometimes, duplication of steps. Someone needed to coordinate. A new role was born, out of necessity. Our production step was to get an airplane into the sky. But this new role wasn't a production role. This new role was to make sure the airplane got off the gate at its departure time and landed at its arrival time. This role was to schedule the people, the ground equipment, the in-flight catering, the aircraft, all at the same time. This was not a production role, but a coordinating role.

"It was *my* new job," Jim said. "For the first time, I was no longer in the cockpit. I was in the background, behind the scenes, working with schedules and checklists, conducting daily huddles, to make sure our planes flew on schedule.

"The output of that project, creating those checklists, making the schedules and defining our methods, allowed us to create a consistent training program. So, as we brought more team members on board, our capacity increased without the chaos. The noise went away. There was a method to our madness and that method was placed in a three ring binder, up on the shelf. It was our Standard Operating Procedures, our Best Practice Book. To solve most problems, we just had to match the problem in the manual and implement the solution.

"Our flight schedules came back in line and our team leaned into the increased passenger load with confidence, based on reality. Things began to work smoother. We had training for new hires. Life was fun again.

Organizational Growth					
Level	Time Span Outlook	Organizational Characteristics	Organizational Challenge	Management Challenge	Necessary Focus
II	3-12m	Headcount increases, reactive behavior toward markets	Sales volume strains operational capacity, pursuit of more sales volume, difficulty for org to focus.	Struggle to delegate while maintaining standards.	Define and document production methods and processes.
I	1d-3m	High risk of sustainability	Negative cash flow	Little or no management depth	Make sales. Introduce product or service into the market. Find a customer, any customer, to buy.

"And then we got a call from our bank," Jim said, shaking his head. Fran nodded, with an understanding smile.

Level III

As the evening wore on, Jim and Fran commiserated about the growing pains of a young enterprise.

"When the bank wants to have a meeting in *your* office, it's fun." Jim's usual grin turned neutral. "When the bank wants to have a meeting in *their* office, it's not fun. And the bank controlled the schedule. I was to report to their office at the appointed time, or risk cancellation of our line of credit." A wince of pain crept into Jim's face as he told the story.

"But, I had a dilemma. I could not abandon my supervisor post and go to the bank. I had to make sure our planes flew.

"At the time, I think it was panic. I looked around for someone to stand in my place, even for the short afternoon. After all, we had planes in the sky.

"It had to be someone who could see beyond today's flight schedule, further into the future," he described. "It had to be someone who could stand a bit of uncertainty. It had to be someone who could effectively work at a higher level than the rest of the crew, someone who could look down the road, anticipate problems and make decisions.

"That is when I discovered George. I mean, I already identified George as a team leader. He was the go-to guy in his group, and more. George would often point out problems in the flight schedule before things went wrong. He would knock on my door and announce that we would be short a pilot on a route three weeks out. He had a sense, an awareness for things that would likely happen next week or next month.

"George had a knack for knowing which team member was having car trouble or a spat with a spouse. 'We have a problem with the schedule, because of a problem at home,' he would say. He didn't make an excuse, he didn't cover up. He took it in stride, made the adjustment and moved on.

"And George would dig through file cabinets looking at maintenance manuals. He would tell me, 'Boss, I know we need to hang onto this flight schedule, but if we keep running these planes like this, they are going to break.' I asked him if he was sure, and he showed me the details on preventive maintenance. He didn't whine, he always had backup for decisions we needed to make." Jim's face relaxed, Fran shifted to pay closer attention.

"So, George was my man. I told everyone, while I was away, George was in charge. And, when I returned late in the afternoon, back from my meeting with the bank, that's the way things stayed. George was in charge, from that day forward.

"It was a good thing George could stand in, to make sure our planes were in the air, because my meeting with the bank didn't go so well. I thought I was a big shot. Our sales were growing, so I asked for a larger line of credit. I thought I was important.

"I can read body language," Jim explained. "When I walked into the plush conference room at the bank, my self-importance shriveled in an instant. My loan officer stood up, shook my hand, introduced me to someone from special assets and left the room. I knew I was special, but special assets have nothing to do with being special. This guy was from the bank's work-out department. His name was Mike Hammermill. I was in trouble and about to be schooled by the master.

"He explained something called 'burn-rate,' which is different from interest rate. He wasn't at all impressed with our hard work, our dedication, our customer following, or popularity on social media. I explained that our increase in flights and new routes outstripped our cash. Our operating costs were up and our suppliers had already extended terms.

"Mike read a paragraph from our loan agreement, the bank could accelerate the interest rate and call the note. Our line of credit was done, cooked. No more grace periods, no more extensions. Funny, he was calm, matter of fact, said he would do me a favor. He rolled our line of credit into a term loan. Our first payment was due in thirty days.

"Mike closed his binder, asked if I would like to have my parking stub validated for the parking garage. I lost a $500,000 line of credit, but I didn't have to pay for parking. That was it. He left me sitting at the table, alone."

Alone With a White Board

"When I got back to the office, I avoided the buzz around the terminal building. I avoided George. Mike Hammermill left me alone at the bank. I was still alone. I knew if I went to my office, someone would corner me with a scheduling question, and at the time, scheduling was not the right question. Toward the end of the hall, in our conference room, was a small white board. That's where I found myself sitting, staring.

"Our financial statements showed an operating loss. I justified that we were a start-up and as long as we could tap our line of credit, we could make payroll and things would work out. But, now, there was no line of credit, payroll was next week and things had to work out. Now."

Fran smiled. She knew this story well.

"It was necessary to make a profit," Jim nodded. "I started to draw on the white board, flowcharting our production sequence. It was like smashing a beer can on my forehead. Obvious unnecessary expenses popped off the board. Over time, our maintenance engineers built in redundant steps. We had quality bottlenecks where a half-finished inspection got stuck waiting for a sign-off. We bought parts on a schedule, but, moved and stored those parts five or six times before they were actually used.

"I always wondered why an aircraft was scheduled for preventive maintenance at our busiest time. Some of our employees worked overtime and some had nothing to do. And when one plane was off schedule, it impacted the positioning of other aircraft. It was very expensive to fly an empty plane because it ended up overnight in the wrong city. Somehow, scrambling, we managed to meet most of our flight schedules, but our cost structure was more than our revenue.

"I knew we were in difficulty, but as I drew this picture on the white board, my attitude changed, I was encouraged. This was not just a problem solving activity, this was fun. I looked at the picture and imagined how to run things smoother by rearranging the work flow. Could we be more efficient if we did preventive maintenance during slow times, rather than busy times?

"This was going to be a big job, but I could see the future. I could see the value in being more efficient. My first goal was to pull 30 percent of the cost out of flight operations. We could make more money when our planes, all four of them, were in the air, than when they were on the ground."

Fran listened to the story, politely. She knew Jim thought he made a brilliant discovery. To her, this was all predictable. This was just a transition, solving one set of problems to step up to the next predictable set of problems.

But, Jim was in the zone. He was no longer sitting in this posh Denver restaurant. His story moved him back, more than twenty-five years, in front of this white board with a flowchart, gathering details.

"The hallway was quiet when I stepped out for some fresh air. Buried in the flowchart, time slipped by. I texted my wife, Susan, a couple of times, so she wouldn't worry. My watch said 9:30pm. Things were bad, but not desperate. Time to go home.

"Susan, met me at the door. She asked how things went with the bank. I told her I had a new loan officer named Hammermill. I said he must have liked me, because, though he pulled a $500,000 line of credit, he didn't make me pay for parking."

Jim stopped. Telling the story surfaced the same emotions from years ago. He leaned back in his chair, then leaned in to the table.

"I got to the office early the next morning. You know sleep is overrated," Jim said. "I intended to go over my flowchart with George, but, first, I needed to fix part of the sequence on the white board. George was already standing in the conference room.

'Are you thinking about making some changes around here?' George asked me. I nodded, yes.

'Looks good,' George said, 'because I have been talking to some of the maintenance teams, and they're concerned. They feel, they are working too hard to get the planes out of maintenance and into the air on schedule. There doesn't seem to be a system. Every problem is a new problem, even if it's the same problem we had last week.'

"Like another beer can on the forehead, it came to me," Jim shook his head from side to side. "I didn't have to draw this flowchart by myself. There was detail that George could help with, and some of the technicians could help George. That would free me up. We had to work quickly, get costs under control, and squeak out enough profit in the next four weeks to make the first payment to the bank on our new term loan." Jim had to laugh as he realized he was not the first CEO with difficulty making a loan payment.

"Our sales volume was up, our customers liked us," Jim proclaimed. "Our airline brand was a success." He paused. "And, we lost money on every ticket. It couldn't be, but as we built the flowchart in the conference room, it became apparent why we were running out of cash. Not our cash, but, the bank's cash. Profit was elusive.

"During the next 24 hours, we convened all kinds of meetings. At first, we thought we should raise our prices, but we confirmed that our competitors had the same fare on the same routes. It was our guess they probably lost money too. And where their price was *below* our price, they must be buying our customers. At the same time, our engineers hyped our airline experience as superior in quality. They argued our customers just didn't appreciate the added logistics and creature comforts embedded in the way we ran our flights.

"We broke the eleventh commandment," Jim said. *"Thou shalt not kid thyself."*

Fran nodded in agreement.

"Turns out, our competition was eating our lunch fair and square," Jim continued. "We were inefficient. Our competitors were more efficient. Even our Mission Statement added unnecessary costs by *exceeding our customers' expectations.* We baked needless costs into the pie.

"With the help of every team, we flowcharted our system, step by step, 180 steps to be exact. Multiple bottlenecks and duplicated effort appeared on the chart. If anything, our design engineers were highly skilled at over-complicating the simplest process. It took two weeks to identify the biggest mud suckers in this chaos and two months to fix them. There were fits and sputters, but we managed.

"Our biggest bottleneck remained, too much ground time," Jim explained. "It's easy to spot a bottleneck, because work always piles up in front of it. Our pileup was an expensive plane parked at the gate, preventing the next plane from getting to that same gate. Planes make money only when they are in the air. So, we made a big change and focused on our gates. Keep the planes in the sky and keep the gates clear. Gates are too expensive to buy more gates. We organized everything around gates.

"Funny, we were most efficient when some of our work teams were idle. As long as we fed the gates, output was predictable and allowed us to schedule everything else more effectively and profitably. Our direct costs came down and everything ran smoother.

"Our new-found profitability freed up financial resources for more R&D. We discovered our gates actually had more capacity, so we fed more budget to our marketing department, added two more people in group sales. It was six months down the road from that first flowchart, but we chugged ahead. The birds sang and the sky turned blue."

Organizational Growth					
Level	Time Span Outlook	Organizational Characteristics	Organizational Challenge	Management Challenge	Necessary Focus
III	1-2y	Awareness of need to become profitable	Competition, costs, profitability	Efficiency	Create systems for efficiency and predictability
II	3-12m	Headcount increases, reactive behavior toward markets	Sales volume strains operational capacity, pursuit of more sales volume, difficulty for org to focus	Struggle to delegate while maintaining standards.	Define and document production methods and processes.
I	1d-3m	High risk of sustainability	Negative cash flow	Little or no management depth	Make sales. Introduce product or service into the market. Find a customer, any customer, to buy.

"That's when we hit the wall again."

Level IV

"We thought there was chaos in the early days, just trying to keep airplanes in the air and our gates clear. Those days were long since behind us, but chaos was creeping back. It was subtle this time. On the surface, things appeared rosy, but, behind the rosy picture, were hidden complications. Meetings went well, efficient in their pace, but sticky problems lingered. You can tell a team is trapped when they continue to deal with the same problem over and over again.

"In a typical meeting, there was an official agenda. If there was no agenda, there was no meeting. But, underneath the official agenda, each participant had a hidden agenda, seeking budget, power and attention. These hidden agendas were slyly introduced and on the surface, appeared to support productivity. Personality conflicts emerged. There were breakdowns in communication, preventable mis-steps in hand-offs from one department to another. Short of name-calling, blame bounced around, depending on who was the goat of the day.

"We hired consultants. To solve our communication difficulties, we sponsored a company-wide communication seminar. To learn to work better as a team, we took personality assessments. We even conducted an in-house workshop on fixing accountability."

"And?" Fran asked.

"Nothing changed," Jim replied. "Waste of time. We were stumped. The company was more complex, with more moving parts. Five years down the road, in our young company, I began to wonder if we were doomed to this dysfunctional group dynamic.

"I asked myself, why? Why did my teams behave this way? Like a group of kids clamoring for attention, each department cared only about itself. To heck with the other guy. Their only focus was internal, narcissistic. 'If our children go to battle and one must die, better yours than mine.'

"And then it occurred to me. I *told* them to behave this way. I told each person, each department, they had to be internally efficient and profitable. No internal waste, no scrap. I commanded high utilization of our precious internal resources. I *told* them to be internally focused.

"It was that *internal* focus that created the next level of organizational friction. Each manager on the executive team managed a department. I told each department to be efficient. The pursuit of departmental efficiency, without regard to other departments, killed the enterprise. I created silos. If we were to survive, all of my departments, divisions, systems and sub-systems had to be integrated into a WHOLE system.

"You see," Jim explained. "There were times when sales outstripped capacity to meet our customer bookings. We thought it was simple enough just to count the seats on a plane. But, we still have weight limits. Can you imagine what it is like to tell a passenger with a confirmed seat that they have to get off the aircraft because the plane is overweight? Or to pull overweight luggage off the loading conveyor, especially when that luggage is ski equipment headed to Denver for a ski vacation?

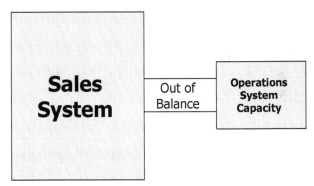

"There were other times when we had more capacity than we could sell. Planes don't make money when they fly half empty. To fill the seats, we lowered the price, but lowering the price decreased our margins.

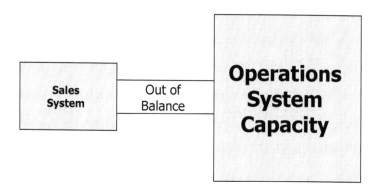

"These cycles of feast and famine killed us. Each cycle allowed our competitors to take a little more market share. We had to balance our systems together. We worked hard on this system-sub-system integration until we got it right.

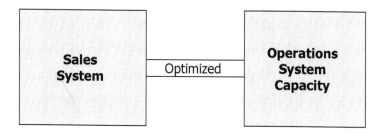

"Things got better, the silos went away. The systems in each department were distinct, but, now, integrated and balanced. We were successful once again.

			Organizational Growth		
Level	Time Span Outlook	Organizational Characteristics	Organizational Challenge	Management Challenge	Necessary Focus
IV	2-5y	Expansion of branches, maturity of operating departments	Friction among operating departments, silos, alignment issues	Balance of systems for total throughput. Finding and training new managers.	Integration of systems and sub-systems into a whole system.
III	1-2y	Awareness of need to become profitable	Competition, costs, profitability	Efficiency	Create systems for efficiency and predictability
II	3-12m	Headcount increases, reactive behavior toward markets	Sales volume strains operational capacity, pursuit of more sales volume, difficulty for org to focus	Struggle to delegate while maintaining standards.	Define and document production methods and processes.
I	1d-3m	High risk of sustainability	Negative cash flow	Little or no management depth	Make sales. Introduce product or service into the market. Find a customer, any customer, to buy.

"But, our success was short-lived." Jim dropped his eyes. "I noticed our trend reports, specifically our rate-of-change indicator moved down. We were still growing, year over year, but, not as fast. And, our competitors seemed to suffer, too. It wasn't just us. Something happened to our passenger market."

Level V

"While our internal systems were balanced and integrated, our passenger market turned anemic. It was a thundering insight that something outside of the company, an *external* system, was as important as any of our internal systems," Jim leaned forward. "It was not enough to push our product into the passenger market, we had to produce something people wanted. It was almost like we started over again. We had to become market responsive. What our passenger market wanted last year, was no longer what they wanted this year. Our passenger market moved. Our growth trended down because we were out of sync with the market. We could figure out the problem, or we could die. Survival was optional."

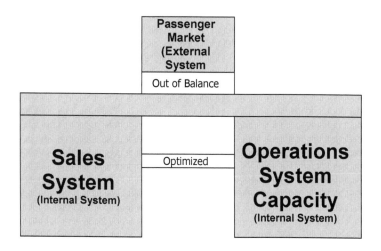

"Running the airline *we* wanted to run only allowed us to grow so big. To continue to grow, we had to run the airline that our *customers* wanted to fly. It was necessary to create a clear and compelling vision of an airline that was relevant to our passenger market. Not just today, not just tomorrow, but constantly adapting. Our passenger market dragged us, kicking and screaming, into the future."

Fran smiled again. She understood it was necessary to pay attention to the *wants* and *needs* of the market, no matter the business.

"And?" she prompted.

"Our internal competence was not enough. We first hired a consultant, a self-proclaimed expert in our industry. Turned out, he was only capable of sharing his limited past experience with us, for a fee. We really needed someone to study our market trends, analyze the patterns in those trends and provide some future direction. As our passenger markets changed, we had to adapt.

Passenger Markets	
Lowest Price	Competitive Price
Vacation and fun	Business and productivity
Fly any time of day (based on price)	Fly at specific times (based on appointment)
Fly with lots of baggage	Fly with minimal baggage
Flexible schedule	Fixed schedule
Coach	Business class

"My role changed," Jim said. "Life as a risk-taking entrepreneur shifted to a more conservative business unit president. I had to look both inside the organization (internal systems) and outside at the passenger market (external system). And everyone counted on me. I always saw myself as a leader, and now that leadership carried great weight. A hundred families depended on the decisions I made each day. Our annual payroll became our monthly payroll. Our competitors could take our market share, or we could take market share from our competitors. It was necessary to get in sync with our passenger market. How does that song go?

Out of sync is out of sight,
Out of sight is out of mind, and
Out of mind is out of business, baby[ii]

"To clearly understand the company, I learned to read financial statements. I always had a soft place in my heart for accounting folks and, now, I knew why. It was easy to get lost in the weeds of day-to-day problems, but I had to make sense of the larger issues that influenced the financial health of our internal systems through time. And, the profit-loss statement only told part of the story. I had to be the steward of our long term resources, our assets. I had to learn about the balance sheet.

"Understanding the balance sheet helped me understand the conversation with Mike Hammermill, from the bank. Not only was he concerned about our profit and loss, but he was concerned about our long term resources, equipment, depreciation, accounts receivable, short term and long term debt. I could no longer run the company by my gut, I had to understand the numbers.

"Things got better. We paid the term loan back. Hammermill moved us out of special assets and turned our account over to a new loan officer. We moved our headquarters from Dickinson, North Dakota to Denver. We had a new line of credit, bigger, but now under much more control, finally," Jim chuckled.

"As I looked at the industry trends, I had to look further into the future." Jim said. "What would change, five years out? The future seemed foggy and uncertain. One thing was crystal clear, five years would pass. Time is relentless."

Organizational Growth					
Level	Time Span Outlook	Organizational Characteristics	Organizational Challenge	Management Challenge	Necessary Focus
V	5-10y	Legacy systems slow, organizational change and adaptation lags market demands.	Sustaining the machine, misplaced dependency on diminishing legacy sales.	Balance of internal operating systems with external market systems	Create a clear and compelling vision that remains relevant and nimble to a shifting market.
IV	2-5y	Expansion of branches, maturity of operating departments	Friction among operating departments, silos, alignment issues	Balance of systems for total throughput. Finding and training new managers.	Integration of systems and sub-systems into a whole system.
III	1-2y	Awareness of need to become profitable	Competition, costs, profitability	Efficiency	Create systems for efficiency and predictability
II	3-12m	Headcount increases, reactive behavior toward markets	Sales volume strains operational capacity, pursuit of more sales volume, difficulty for org to focus	Struggle to delegate while maintaining standards.	Define and document production methods and processes.
I	1d-3m	High risk of sustainability	Negative cash flow	Little or no management depth	Make sales. Introduce product or service into the market. Find a customer, any customer, to buy.

Level VI

It was Fran's turn to talk. She explained that the Coriolis portfolio contained seven companies. Fran worked closely, not only with her investor board, but seven entrepreneurs just like Jim. Each business unit was related to the airline industry, but none were direct competitors in the same market. Coriolis assembled this portfolio by looking at market trends more than ten years into the future. Outbound Air would be their first airline.

"What do you look for, ten years into the future?" Jim asked.

"Long range trends," Fran replied. "We understand that specific details fade into the background, but, conceptually, we think air travel will continue to grow. We don't know who the players might be, but look at this long term cycle." Fran pulled a small paper pad out of her satchel and drew a picture.

"There are ten major airlines around the world," she sketched, "and dozens of small airlines. To compete, major airlines buy small airlines and eventually each other. As these airlines consolidate their routes and gates, the passenger market splinters. There is confusion. In that turmoil, new small regional airlines find an underserved passenger market and buy some of the leftover gates. The small regional airline gets traction and the cycle repeats itself."

"But, how do you plan out ten years?" Jim asked.

"One of the trends we see, is a move to smaller jets with scheduled service into smaller markets. Eight years ago, buying our first airline was a ten year strategy. We didn't know Outbound Air, but we knew there would be someone like Outbound Air that we might buy. We studied companies like Embraer and Bombardier, manufacturing aircraft with passenger loads of 70-90 people. We believe if we can fill seats on planes traveling to smaller markets, we can make good profits and expand. There are a number of smaller markets that simply won't support a Boeing 737 with 140 seats, but those markets *can* support scheduled service with smaller jets." Fran stopped to make sure Jim followed the logic of the business model.

"We know Outbound has a mixed fleet of Dash-8s and other prop planes," she continued, "but if a passenger has an alternative, jets are faster and can fly farther. That's why we were attracted to you. With our capital, we think Outbound Air can make the transition to jets."

Organizational Growth

Level	Time Span Outlook	Organizational Characteristics	Organizational Challenge	Management Challenge	Necessary Focus
VI	10-20y	Portfolio company that leverages the capability of its individual business units to maximize profits in long term market cycles. Both private and public companies.	Cultural integration of acquired companies. Branding of individual products or services in a portfolio of independent business units. Government regulation.	Finding executive talent with the capability to identify and effectively work in conceptual market value chains.	Macro-markets and long term trends to leverage large scale markets on a national or emerging international scope. Attention to market perception and social stewardship.
V	5-10y	Legacy systems slow, organizational change and adaptation lags market demands.	Sustaining the machine, misplaced dependency on diminishing legacy sales.	Balance of internal operating systems with external market systems	Create a clear and compelling vision that remains relevant and nimble to a shifting market.
IV	2-5y	Expansion of branches, maturity of operating departments	Friction among operating departments, silos, alignment issues	Balance of systems for total throughput. Finding and training new managers.	Integration of systems and sub-systems into a whole system.
III	1-2y	Awareness of need to become profitable	Competition, costs, profitability	Efficiency	Create systems for efficiency and predictability
II	3-12m	Headcount increases, reactive behavior toward markets	Sales volume strains operational capacity, pursuit of more sales volume, difficulty for org to focus	Struggle to delegate while maintaining standards.	Define and document production methods and processes.
I	1d-3m	High risk of sustainability	Negative cash flow	Little or no management depth	Make sales. Introduce product or service into the market. Find a customer, any customer, to buy.

Jim kept up with Fran as she described how Outbound Air might fit with Coriolis. Up to now, Jim saw Outbound Air as a large, mature company against a smattering of small charter operators. But, it was all about perspective. His big, mature company was only a small player in a larger universe. He leaned forward in his chair.

"I feel like I am back at the beginning again," Jim said. "Almost like startup mode, but in a much bigger way."

Fran's board of directors planned this airline acquisition eight years earlier. They slowly put companies together according to a long-term conceptual plan. They would not likely see the fruits of their labor for another eight years. So many things could go wrong.

"But if things go right," Fran explained, "Coriolis is in the market to be acquired."

Jim shifted in his chair. It was a long term gamble. The reality of it, and his part in it, made him feel uneasy. His high interest was balanced by fear. What might happen to his company? It was an uncertain and ambiguous future.

Part Three

Make Everyone Think Like an Owner

Al Ripley had a problem. Since he brought in his hand-picked management team, the existing Outbound employees were suspect about their new leader and nervous about their own job security. Before the merger, Jim Dunbar did his best to prepare the troops for any discomfort through the transition period. But, no one prepared them for the quirky mannerisms of Al Ripley.

The level of trust was low, uncertain skepticism. Ripley's expectations shifted on a whim. Often, the shift seemed intentional, just to keep people off-balance.

George was one of the first in the cross-hairs, a target who needed to learn the new world order of corporate life according to Ripley.

"No more Mr. Nice Guy," George was told. "I need you to think like an owner, make decisions like an owner, and solve problems like an owner. I want you to feel like this company is as much yours, as it is mine," Al announced at the start of every team meeting.

George thought about that. Yes, instill a sense of ownership. Own the problem, own the solution. But, yet, it was only a *sense* of ownership, not *real* ownership.

George talked about this to some of the pilots. "Who are you kidding?" they said. "It's not my plane. It's the company's plane." George allowed that it was only an analogy, not really ownership, but stewardship. The pilots just laughed. "The new CEO wants us to think like an owner. We'll show him what ownership thinking is all about."

George shrugged his shoulders as he left the discussion. Soon he found out what the pilots had in mind.

> **Pilot Andrew Johnson,**
> Left seat decision maker,
> Thinking like an owner of
> Embraer N-8919.
> Announces the sale of his
> aircraft.
> Please follow this link to EBay.

The flyer on the bulletin board displayed a selfie portrait of Andrew Johnson next to his Outbound jet. George chuckled as he walked away. "Now, that's thinking like an owner," he said to himself.

Al Ripley, however, was none too pleased. Andrew Johnson was summarily dismissed two days later. There was no more talk about thinking like an owner.

Flattening the Organization

Al Ripley believed, for every management problem, there was a management consultant. As issues surfaced in meetings, Al would look down his nose, over the top rim of his glasses, and ask the inevitable. "Don't we know a consultant that can help us with that?"

Those meetings were short and decisive. Ripley emerged from the conference room victorious, confident that he met adversity with a firm commitment to the solution, by hiring a consultant.

Some problems, however, did not go away. But then, Al quickly pointed out, "We must have hired the wrong consultant."

One organizational guru, Preston Pratney, promised to save the company several hundred thousand dollars. He charged no fee, and only took a pro-rated amount from the savings he created. No savings, no pro-rated fee.

"If you really want to save on overhead, you have to cut salaries that make a dent in the bottom line," Pratney said. Outbound lost an entire middle layer of management that week.

"Don't let go of your production people," he warned. "You still need someone to do the work. But a lot of this supervision and middle management can go. It's all about empowerment. We are going to drive decision making down to the front lines. After all, they are closest to the customer, they should be able to figure things out on their own."

Self-Directed Work Teams

"In fact, we are going to call them self-directed work teams," Preston Pratney decreed. He pulled out a tattered magazine article. "See here, this company uses self-directed work teams. This is a new age, where hierarchy is outdated. Empowerment is the key."

Empowerment became the answer to all problems of productivity and accountability. "E" posters decorated the hallways.

At first, the middle managers and supervisors weren't missed. Flight operations, one day, seemed to carry on like the day before. Departure schedules were locked in. Standard purchase agreements were followed with suppliers. Customer credit cards cleared the bank. Perhaps Preston Pratney was right.

That first year saved $730,000 in salaries and overhead. Preston Pratney was happy with his take-home pay. Divided in half, he hauled in a cool $365,000 for his efforts. No wonder he was upbeat when he arrived every Monday to go over his spreadsheet of savings.

Self-directed work groups also solved another problem in long term wage-management. No one dared aspire to become a supervisor, because all supervisors were excommunicated. Granted, most self-directed work teams had a team leader, but the role came with no increase in pay. Every person on the team had the same authority. Accountability fell to the group with no team member singled out for performance standards.

Self-directed work teams completely eliminated accountability conversations. Since no single person was accountable for underperformance, no VP needed to confront the guilty. Underperformance was always addressed as a group motivational speech. The root cause of a process problem was rarely discussed, or identified, or explored, or resolved. This included the inevitable slippage of on-time departures.

"As you know, Outbound Air, under the leadership of Al Ripley, now embraces self-directed work teams," Preston Pratney smiled, in advance of the bad news. "We discovered that our on-time departures slipped by an average of 32 minutes in the past two months. It is our policy, here at Outbound, to empower employees to solve these problems, so, that is the purpose of this meeting. We know that each of you is well-intentioned, but it is obvious that we all have to try a little bit harder to get these planes out on time. If there are any questions, please come and see me. You know we have an open door policy around here." Pratney's face beamed at the group as he left the room.

But, days that work out, just like the day before, eventually come to a halt.

It was Wednesday afternoon. Hump day. Everyone skated through, waiting for the weekend. In most back rooms, out of view of the customer, hung 24-hour flat panel weather monitors. This rectangular chorus routinely marched the weather in brilliant colors across the map, from left to right, waves of green, pockmarked with yellows and reds. In winter, clearly defined by the ridges of the Rocky Mountains, those green rain bands turned to light blue snow showers, occasionally, dark blue blizzards. Mixed sleet and ice showed up in shades of magenta.

But, in aviation, weather is seldom an event, more often a process. A dark band of rain could hold together, or break apart.

At 2:00p, the process began. The color green filled the upper left quadrant of each screen. It was mostly pilots who paid attention, checking and double-checking their flight plans. By 2:30p, small groups began to assemble in front of each screen. Public-facing departure monitors switched ON-TIME status to DELAYED. DELAYED status was not unusual for Outbound as its average departure time continued to slip in between bouts of improvement.

But, the switch from DELAYED to CANCELLED was the trigger that set off the customer service lines. This weather system was not particularly strong, but the temperatures were borderline freezing. A little colder would have yielded consistent snow, not a terrific problem, but freezing rain and sleet along with a small drop in temperatures grounded half of Outbound's fleet.

Pilots headed for the nearest hotel. Customer service agents logged a little overtime. Though the schedule was interrupted, most Outbound employees were happy. Another day, not quite like yesterday, but with the promise that tomorrow things would be back to normal.

Except, the planes that were supposed to be in Denver, still sat in Dickinson, and the planes destined for Kansas City were grounded in Jasper.

Thursday morning, all the self-directed work teams showed up to a decidedly different situation. Some passengers spent the night in the airport, other passengers carpooled from a local hotel. They all wanted answers.

The first departure from Dickinson was scheduled for Denver. Only one person climbed the stairs to the aircraft door. Twenty-eight people were stuck in Kansas City with their plane in Jasper. The pilots did their pilot thing and the customer service reps did their best to keep people calm, but no one could make a decision about airplanes stranded in the wrong place. It took three working days and some renegade decisions to get things back in place.

Preston Pratney conducted a series of conference calls to address the situation. "First, we want to thank everyone who pitched in to work overtime. That's what we mean, when we empower our employees to do the right thing. I know it's been a bit confusing over the past three days, but the weather is something totally out of our control, couldn't be helped. We won't make excuses for it. We have to keep our eyes focused forward. So, we learned some hard lessons during this storm and just want to encourage everyone to try a little harder the next time this happens. In the meantime, if you have questions, shoot me an email. You know my door is always open."

Chief Culture Officer

If you put a frog into boiling water, it makes a frantic attempt to leap out. If you put a frog in cold water and slowly bring it to a boil, it succumbs to the gradual shift in temperature until it expires. It's an old management analogy, but that was the analogy on Jim Dunbar's mind.

He could see, from his corner office, all the changes around him. The teamwork posters on the wall, thinking like an owner, self-directed work teams, all had the appearance of positive change. But something was off-balance. Jim couldn't put his finger on it. His memory told him that he faced these challenges before, that he solved these problems before. In the early days of Outbound Air, Jim never thought much about teamwork posters, every team had a manager and there was never any question about who owned the company.

In spite of Ripley's workshop on *Make Decisions Like an Owner,* from Jim's experience, he knew what it felt like to own a company and now, he knew what it felt like to work for Al Ripley. It did not feel the same.

Ropes Course

At times, Al Ripley took things in his own hands. As morale teetered back and forth, he arrived at the conclusion that some team building was in order. "Don't we know a consultant who can help us with that?" he challenged his VP group.

As luck would have it, there was a training facility out of Bismarck, North Dakota that specialized in team building. Bismarck was only a short hop from Dickinson, so, a resident consultant shuttled all Outbound personnel on a rotating basis for three days of team-building at Ropes, Inc.

Jason, the sales rep for Ropes, Inc., described their operation. "Our company started out designing and building zip lines and climbing structures," he smiled. For a zip line tour, Ropes, Inc. could only charge $75 a person. Then, they stumbled into leadership programs. Branding their zip line tour as a leadership program, they could charge $250 a person, and their customers arrived in groups. Teambuilding, they called it. Ropes, Inc. expanded into tug-o-war and even built a mud pit.

"How many people in your party?" Jason asked.

Marsha Feldman was Outbound's head of HR. "I want you to put them through the wringer," she directed. "I know we have some bad apples in our group and I want you to expose them."

"That's what we do here," Jason replied. "We put your teams under pressure. They will either crack or weld together. Everything becomes visible. We have people who jump and high-five, and people who break down and cry."

Profiles Anonymous

At the executive management level, Al Ripley cleaned house from the governance of Jim Dunbar, but today, he could only shake his head. Fresh off the battlefield at Ropes, Inc., Marsha Feldman worked hard to press her new influence as VP of Human Resources. Based on her observations of the self-directed work teams in the ropes course and the mud pit, she was adamant that Rafael, in operations, had no respect for women.

She cornered Ripley after the weekly VP meeting. "Mr. Ripley, you hired me to handle our Human Resources, and it's a big job. You understand the liability we face these days if we don't treat our employees right. And that goes the same for some of our senior managers. I talked to you about Rafael before. I know he ranks higher on the org chart than me, but when I call a meeting to discuss our diversity program and sensitivity training, I expect him to, at least, have the courtesy to pretend he takes my role seriously."

Ripley took a long breath and asked for more details. "I can't make a decision based solely on your opinion. I will need more information." Ripley did not actually want more information, he just wanted Marsha to go away.

"Well, this is not an isolated incident," Marsha replied. "Rafael consistently ignores directives from my HR department. He has no respect for me or my team. One of these days, his behavior is going to backfire and his treatment of other employees will land us in a lawsuit."

Truth be told, Al Ripley did not have much respect for Marsha either, not because she was a woman, but because he had disdain for the role of HR.

"HR is like a complaint department," he declared, with Marsha out of the room. "When you open up a complaint department, people start complaining."

Even with Marsha in the room, Ripley's attitude was thinly disguised. Whenever Marsha spoke, Ripley rolled his eyes. Rafael was able to ignore Marsha's directives because Ripley not only condoned that behavior, but subtly endorsed it. Ripley felt like a babysitter, two kids in the sandbox, neither playing well with the other.

"I have come to the conclusion," Marsha said, "that Rafael and I just don't mix. We are like oil and water."

"So, what do you suppose we should do about it?" Ripley shook his head.

"I have been doing some research on personality profiles. I believe we need to do an assessment on everyone who works here, so we can find out why they behave the way they do. I found a consultant that is willing to come in, administer the assessments, help us interpret the results and recommend ways to fix some of our obvious dysfunctions."

"And, just exactly *when* would we do all of this?" Al asked. "We chewed up a lot of productivity with that team building thing. We have an airline to run. Do we really have the time to run around playing amateur psychologist?"

"Oh, that is just the start of it," Marsha countered. "Based on what the assessments tell us about Rafael and the rest of his team, I think we should host a communication seminar and a series of leadership workshops. Human Resources is a big job. This company is growing larger and we have to become more professional."

Motivational Speakers

Jim Dunbar arrived early each morning. It was a habit he adopted early on, as a pilot. "The last thing a pilot wants to be, is in a hurry," Jim would say. "Better to be an hour early than one minute late."

Jim set his favorite coffee mug on its coaster, propped open his laptop and scanned his email.

URGENT was the only word in the subject line from its sender, Al Ripley.

URGENT

Jim. I am dismayed at the morale in this company. And as Chief Culture Officer, I hold you accountable. See me in my office at 9a sharp.

-Ripley

Jim sighed as he archived the email. He took a sip from his mug and set out to Ripley's office. Al Ripley was not really dismayed, but it served him to sound upset when he wanted to get his way without a great deal of discussion.

"Jim, you know Marsha Feldman in HR, the new girl?" Ripley asked.

Jim nodded his head. Before Coriolis, Jim never felt the need to have a Human Resources Department. His managers were always in charge of personnel planning for their own departments, hiring and firing. But, as the company grew, perhaps it was inevitable.

"Our people are our biggest asset," Ripley continued, "and Marsha Feldman says morale stinks. She wants to conduct some employee climate survey, has a consultant that will cost us $20,000. I don't know what she needs a survey for, if she already knows that morale stinks."

Jim looked down, not searching for a response, but to acknowledge that if morale was bad, then the role of Chief Culture Officer should appear contrite.

"Instead of giving her $20,000 to conduct this survey, I am giving you half that amount to find a good motivational speaker. As this company grows, every once in a while, we need to bring in a good speaker to pump up morale."

Jim held his tongue. It didn't feel right, but, maybe this is how a corporation had to run things as it got bigger.

Al wrapped it up. "Don't bother me with the details, just get something scheduled. I want to see video recordings of the top three guys. This has to be a first-class affair. Within budget, of course."

Manipulation

Financial controllers don't often leave their office, but Dolores Gusta discovered something that caught her curiosity. She had orders from Al Ripley to set up an account on the books called *Teambuilding and Morale*. The account had a maximum budget of $10,000 for an event that Jim Dunbar was supposed to plan. To date, expenses were zero.

Today, she got a request from one of the baggage supervisors. The supervisor submitted an expense receipt for a pizza he bought for a crew required to work overtime during a rain storm. This was not an employee meal, which would have been disallowed. The supervisor said it was for morale. In the past, Dolores would have immediately rejected the reimbursement request, but now, she had a new expense category, *Teambuilding and Morale*. The category had a $10,000 budget. The cost for the pizza was only $18, so she did not spend much time deciding one way or the other. Account code 21-383-1038-*Teambuilding and Morale*, done.

In the grand scheme of things, this was immaterial. But at the end of the month, this expense code totaled $2,408. A look at the vendor list showed the likes of Tower of Pizza, Pizza Town and Sicilian Oven. That was a lot of pizza, and the corporation had a strict policy that disallowed employee meals. This would be immaterial in a financial audit, but an egregious violation of company policy, so Dolores had to ask.

Apparently, word spread, true or not, any supervisor could buy pizza for the crew, code the expense to *Teambuilding and Morale* and the reimbursement would be approved. Dolores had to determine, if she would be a whistle-blower hero or a corporate snitch. This could go either way for her.

Dolores pieced things together. The account code was set up for a project under Jim Dunbar with an original budget of $10,000. Within two weeks, almost 25 percent of that budget was eroded by pizza. Dolores worked for Al Ripley in three companies before. She learned her lesson long ago. If anyone was going to take the fall for this, she decided it was Jim Dunbar.

"Hot potato" is a children's game where an object is tossed from one to another as if that object is a "hot potato." Jim Dunbar's door was open when Dolores arrived, but she still gave the courtesy of a knock. She held the "hot potato" in her hand, a one page schedule of pizza expense. In an instant, that "hot potato" was on Jim's desk with only a brief explanation, and Dolores was out the door and down the hall.

Jim was puzzled. Since Al Ripley took over, he had zero contact with the accounting team. Now he was faced with budget oversight on a project that was already eroded by 25 percent. He stared. Jim Dunbar stared at an expense that, by any measure, for a multi-million dollar airline operation was simply silly. But, he knew Al Ripley, and this silliness would cost him the better part of an otherwise upbeat morning.

Jim Dunbar was not one to shy away from confrontation, even if he knew he was on the losing side. No need for an appointment. This was a stupid issue anyway.

"Al. I looked at the budget for this motivational speaker project," Jim began.

"Yes, how is that going? Haven't seen those videos of the speakers you picked out. You making progress on that?" Al interrupted.

"That's not what I came to talk about," Jim was calm. "Delores just gave me a recap of the budget expense on this project. Looks like almost a quarter of the budget was spent on pizza? I thought this budget was for a speaker?"

"Oh, that," Al chortled. "Yeah. I thought it was a good idea to raise morale if the boys would order a little pizza for the crew. You got $10,000 in your budget, you can absorb a couple of pizzas."

"But, someone approved more than a couple of pizzas," Jim explained.

"Look, Jim, I have an airline to run. It's your budget, you're in charge. I hold you accountable for managing your budget. If you can't handle it, then perhaps we can find someone else." Al Ripley paused. "If you are willing to forego your earn-out?"

Their eyes met in a stand-off. Jim was seething, but held check on his emotions. Somehow, Al Ripley managed to reduce his role in the company to a babysitter of pizza.

The speaker event came and went. A headliner adorned the stage at a posh hotel in Denver. It was a smashing success. Those who attended, high-fived each other, chanted a song and learned a secret handshake. People talked about the event the entire next day.

Two weeks later, Marsha Feldman was awarded a $20,000 budget to conduct an employee climate survey. In spite of the motivational speaker, Marsha continued to describe company morale as poor. Six weeks later, the survey reported, in the executive summary, that Outbound Air suffered in the area of leadership which led to communication breakdowns and personality conflicts. The consultant proposed a three month leadership program and included an invoice for the initial retainer.

Ripley rejected the proposal, said the survey was a waste of resources and did not tell him anything he did not already know. Jim Dunbar concluded the company should have spent all the budget on pizza.

Tribal Leadership

Preston Pratney was beside himself. The debacle over stranded aircraft during the string of weather delays and cancellations created pressure on Preston to re-instate some of the dismissed managers. The lost revenue on cancelled flights and aircraft re-positioning cost Outbound more than double the savings from the reduction in middle-management. But, Pratney was undeterred. His consulting fee was calculated on 50 percent of the savings from flight and ground operations. His contract cleverly contained a clause that no losses from weather related incidents would count against the calculations in his fee. So, while the losses mounted, Pratney's fee continued to pay out like a fixed annuity.

Still, the breakdown in decision making created a glaring fracture in the flattened structure he prescribed. Never to let a crisis go to waste, it was time for Preston Pratney to roll out his version of *Tribal Leadership*.

"We learned a lot from the losses the airline took during the weather delays last month," he addressed a group of three teams. "We know you all worked hard, many of you took home a fair share of overtime pay. We have come to the conclusion that working harder, simply isn't enough. Outbound Air is now embarking on a new program called *Tribal Leadership*. In the days before hierarchy, men organized into tribes, and that is how they hunted, with the women as gatherers. There was a tribal chief, but there were no managers or supervisors.

"Hierarchy is dead," Preston proclaimed. "This is the 21st century. The time has come to dismantle the outdated organizations of the industrial age. The time has come to get back to the basic fundamentals of tribes, where people work together, solving their own problems. From now on, consider your work team as your tribe. Each of you is fully responsible. *Tribal Leadership.*"

Incentives

His friends called him "Purse." Daniel Pursemeister was in charge of purchasing for Outbound Air. At age 63, he looked forward to retirement in a couple of years. The date was not set in stone, because, when Daniel looked at his personal savings account, he realized that he was a little short on his retirement goals.

A little short was not entirely accurate. Daniel Pursemeister was just short of broke. A late life divorce forced his home on the real estate market during a down cycle. The phantom equity in his largest asset evaporated in the space between his golden years and divorce court.

But, Daniel was saved by Al Ripley. At least the equity in his house was saved. When Daniel Pursemeister heard about the new company bonus program, he was skeptical. But as events unfolded, his skepticism turned to hope.

Al Ripley surveyed the company and made many judgments about the people on his new team. He looked for leverage, he looked for weakness. Daniel Pursemeister was a buyer, the company Purchasing Manager. Anything the company bought over $5000 in any given year passed across Pursemeister's desk. It didn't take long for Ripley to notice, Daniel needed money. In his employee file, there were two retirement letters, each submitted, then withdrawn. Daniel hoped to retire, but couldn't. He was overextended.

The incentive plan for Daniel was part of a larger bonus program that Ripley developed to handcuff players to his bench. There was logic behind it. Last year's expense budget was the base. Any reduction in expenses over last year went into the pool. The pool would be divided among the managers on a pro-rated basis. Daniel was named into the pool. As Purchasing Manager, he could question all expenses, negotiate with vendors, delay payments to vendors, and substitute products. Daniel could have a direct impact on the bottom line.

And he took his job seriously. At first wind of the bonus pool, he doubted that additional improvements could be made. Until late one Thursday afternoon.

De-icing fluid was a big expense for Outbound. Winters are long in North Dakota, Montana and Wyoming. Further south, the jet stream danced between Utah and Colorado, grazing the Texas panhandle, but, each winter, those northern states remained under a constant polar vortex. In the early days, for de-icing, Outbound Air only used the cheap stuff, orange in color. Across a five state region, on an average winter day, there were rarely more than a couple dozen take-offs, the time lapse between de-icing and wheels up, seldom more than five minutes. With a fifteen minute window, the orange fluid did the trick.

When Outbound leased its fifteenth plane, things changed, and there was a management decision to shift from the orange fluid to the green fluid. This decision opened the take-off window from a maximum of 15 minutes to a minimum of 30 minutes, and under the right conditions, the hold-over time to take-off could be extended to 80 minutes after de-icing. Of course, this hold-over time had a cost, and cost containment was Daniel Pursemeister's job.

This Thursday afternoon, Daniel discovered that, even though his requisition clearly specified the green fluid, it was the orange fluid that got delivered.

When Daniel picked up the invoice, his fingers slipped and the paper sailed sideways, then back again before it settled underneath the rear of the desk. He grimaced as he slowly slid out of his chair, onto his knees to retrieve the invoice from the darkness underneath. Dust bunnies clearly attached themselves to distract his attention, but the numbers were unmistakable. Orange fluid was cheaper than green fluid. His spine tensed. Any pilot relying on the extended hold-over time to take off could end in disaster. In the daytime, the pilot would be visually alerted by stickers and colored caps on the deicing truck, but at night, orange fluid looked like green fluid.

His eyes darted to the phone. Who should he call? Or should he just issue a memorandum, a safety bulletin? Quick, make a decision.

And, then it occurred to him. Orange fluid was cheaper than green fluid. Any reduction in expense went into his bonus calculation.

Daniel's attention shifted to his computer. He had access to take-off logs. Ten minutes later, he had his answer. Regardless of the de-icing fluid, 100 percent of the take-offs from the Dickinson airport this past winter season occurred within 15 minutes of de-icing. An hour later, he scoured the log for all take-offs during the past thirty days in North Dakota, South Dakota, Wyoming, Idaho and Colorado. He chuckled. Of course. Those airports were so small, there was rarely any traffic, never more than one plane in the take-off cue.

So, the budget paid for green, the cash paid for orange, the difference went into Daniel Pursemeister's bonus pool. Perfect.

Part Four

The Touch

Al Ripley sat alone in his Denver office, staring into the short space between his desk and the door. Behind him, the glow of blue sky created a stark backlight, intentional retina burn to any visitor seated across from him. Be it casual conversation or hard ball negotiation, Ripley's purpose was always the same, cripple the adversary in front and drive them to their knees, even if the conquest was over a nickel in the company football pool.

For the first time since he took over Outbound Air, Al Ripley felt confident, in control. The psychological beating administered to Jim Dunbar over the past months created the needed distance. Ripley did not have to generate high achievement to appear great, only diminish those below. Jim Dunbar was the only challenge left in the takeover, and now that was done.

On his desk was a request. It was a curious request. Representative Orville Hatchmeyer, duly elected from an emerging congressional district in the rich oil land of North Dakota, penned the letter. It was unlike other letters from political figures, promising to make life better, with an extended hand to extract a political donation. This letter was a promise.

Representative Hatchmeyer wanted to leave a legacy. His proposal included a namesake facility, the Hatchmeyer Regional International Airport. Ripley read and re-read the letter, tried to figure out exactly where this airport was, or *if* it was, or if it was *to be*. In the fine print, he finally deciphered, the airport existed in the small town of Dickinson, North Dakota. Dickinson was, indeed, part of a weekly scheduled run for Outbound, a quick in and out. Frequent travelers took the bus, but those with plans on any given Thursday, could buy a ticket on Outbound Air.

Hatchmeyer's proposal was aggressive. Daily jet service in and out of Dickinson. Outbound would receive a substantial federal subsidy to defray the cost of operational load factors below break-even. The Transportation Safety Administration would be given a budget to upgrade airport security. U.S. Customs would establish operating hours, Monday to Friday 8-5 and weekends, by appointment.

When Ripley took over Outbound, he had designs on building the prestige of the airline, moving into marginal markets, just outside a limited number of larger markets. It was a hedging strategy, feeding off the crumbs left by major carriers, just outside the traffic corridors of interest. But, Dickinson? Dickinson was way off the radar.

The letter had all the makings of a horsehead deal. Federal budget for airport upgrades. Subsidized flight operations. But, why?

Al leaned back in his chair, its center of gravity pitched back like a Sunday afternoon Lazyboy. Orville Hatchmeyer lived in Dickinson. To escape his rural empire required a ninety minute drive to the nearest airport in Bismarck, except on Thursday, when he could get scheduled air service on Outbound. Hatchmeyer paid his dues as a small unknown congressional representative, but now, the oil patch was his salvation. North Dakota was suddenly on the map, and Hatchmeyer was suddenly important.

On several occasions, he delivered the tiebreaking vote for some highway exit or a bridge over swampland. Now it was his turn. Like a free upgrade to first class, Hatchmeyer wanted his own airplane. But this was even better, an airport with his name and subsidized air service at taxpayer expense. He wouldn't even have to pay for fuel.

Al Ripley looked at the letter. He thought how important it might be to make a campaign contribution. On second thought, he would have to be careful. There must not be any sense of impropriety. He was certain Hatchmeyer thought the same way. Outbound was never political, never sought political favors, so now, it was the perfect political target.

The Mark

The first meeting between Al Ripley and Orville Hatchmeyer appeared to be by chance. In the guise of a public hearing on an airport zoning matter, Hatchmeyer's staff conducted an inquiry into public response to allow for a hotel concession adjacent to airport property in Dickinson.

It was the kind of hearing that would never make it onto Ripley's radar, much less his calendar. But a handwritten memo, delivered by overnight mail landed on his desk.

> Dear Mr. Ripley,
> Next Thursday, August 22, there will be a public hearing related to the airport property in Dickinson. Does Outbound Air have any interest in the outcome of that hearing?
> Sincerely,
> The desk of Orville Hatchmeyer

Ripley had absolutely no interest in the outcome of the hearing, but the indication that he might have influence definitely caught his attention.

One touch on his telephone summoned his administrative assistant. "Mindy, call this guy back. You won't be able to get through to him, but talk to his aide. Find out what time the hearing is scheduled on Thursday. Whenever the hearing is, tell him that I will be a half an hour late due to a schedule conflict. Tell him, I look forward to meeting Mr. Hatchmeyer. Then book me on our Denver to Dickinson flight leg. I think we still run scheduled service up there on Thursdays."

The Bait

Orville Hatchmeyer began the hearing with all the pomp and circumstance of something way more important. Six people sat in metal folding chairs in an area of the Dickinson airport right outside the coffee shop. The ruse for the gathering concerned a proposal for a hotel on airport property. Indeed, two local mom and pop hoteliers showed up to legitimize the meeting. Orville asked if there was any interest in an exclusive bid for a long term lease at the airport, then announced existing submittals from two national hotel chains. He indicated that he would notify all parties when a decision was made. Fifteen minutes after it began, the meeting adjourned.

The coffee shop sequestered a fresh pot of coffee with their finest Styrofoam cups and set up a small conference room right off the concourse. Hatchmeyer assumed a large stuffed chair in the corner and waited for his appointed guest.

Al Ripley stepped off the plane, immediately ushered into the terminal building. It was his first time at this airport, but all ground personnel were alerted to his arrival. A newspaper reporter assigned to cover the public hearing stepped away to his car, not realizing that the real story of the day was about to unfold.

"Mr. Ripley, so glad you could make it. Unfortunately the hearing concluded a few minutes ago, but I knew you were coming and just wanted to give you the courtesy of my time."

Al Ripley listened, not to the words, but the context of the words. This meeting was only incidental to the cover purpose for the two of them to be in the same room at the same time. If questioned, the subject of their conversation was hotels on airport property.

"Sorry, I was late. My fault. The flight was on time, but I got held up, and since I'm the CEO, they delayed the plane. How did your meeting go? Any local interest on your hotel here?"

"Oh, yes. Local interest," Hatchmeyer explained. "But Marriott has already put in a confidential bid that will take it."

"Marriott?" Ripley questioned. "With all due respect, Dickinson is not that big of a town. Why, we only fly here once a week." Both men tap-danced around what was unofficially on the table. Hatchmeyer wanted daily service to Dickinson. Ripley knew it. More than that, Hatchmeyer wanted an airport with his name on it.

"That's what I want to talk to you about," Orville lowered his voice. Like a secret he was about to spill, his head began to nod. "Marriott is interested. And they know you only fly here once a week. They think if they build their hotel, you would be interested in the business traveler that stays there. Why, you might even decide to fly here a bit more often."

It was a trial balloon, not to see if Ripley had interest, but to see if Ripley would talk about expanded service under the pretense of an arrangement with a brand name hotel. "You see, the oil patch out here is attracting some significant attention," Hatchmeyer continued. "We're even looking at a tie-in with a Canadian outfit scouting for a leg on their pipeline."

"That's so?" Ripley replied. Hook set.

The two gentlemen continued their meeting for another twenty minutes, short of concluding anything definitive. That first meeting was just to see if the other was willing to play the game.

The Sweetener

The next time the two met at a regional tourism conference on transportation in Denver. Once again, the purpose for their meeting was incidental to the real agenda. The only substance of the second meeting was to set a time and place for a third meeting.

The third meeting was scheduled with exclusive intention. Hatchmeyer did not want to meet in Ripley's office and Ripley did not want to travel to Hatchmeyer's Dickinson office. They both needed deniability and settled on neutral ground, the Brown Palace in Denver. They now knew each other's language, both verbal and non-verbal. They both knew the open agenda and the unspoken agenda. This meeting would be different.

"I took a look at those plans from Marriott," Ripley began. Hatchmeyer understood the meaning behind Ripley's words, but he was not prepared for the rest of the sentence. "The plans look pretty standard for a Marriott footprint, but the architect works for a local guy out of Bismarck that owns one of their other branded hotels. My guess, Marriott corporate doesn't even know about this. It's just one of their local operators."

Orville understood everything that Ripley just placed on the table. And Ripley knew that Hatchmeyer knew. So, now the wraps on the conversation could come off and the two could get down to business.

"Do you really care who actually operates the hotel?" Orville asked. "Or, do you just care that it has the name Marriott on the outside? Or, do you just care that it has 200 guestrooms filled with people who want to fly Outbound Air on a daily basis?"

"Mr. Hatchmeyer, you and I both know that just because there is a hotel there, doesn't mean I am going to fill a plane every day. Sure, brand makes a difference, but it will take time and a whole lot of other factors to fill a plane on a daily route out of Dickinson. How do you suggest we handle the shortfall?" Ripley's question contained the assumption of complicity.

"That's why you need me," Orville answered. "Do you know why I am the Congressional representative from the state of North Dakota? Because I make things happen. All those tree-huggers against fracking for oil, they come out to North Dakota, file a little protest. But, we ain't got no trees out there where the oil is. So, guess what? We're fracking for oil. You want a little piss-ant hotel on your airport? Done. I can make it happen. You're worried about a little short-fall on your load factors. I can make it happen." The blood ran hot in Orville's face, his neck seemed to grow thicker. But, Al Ripley was cool.

"And how do you suggest we handle the shortfall?" Ripley repeated.

Orville stopped. "You don't think I know much about running an airline," he tested. "But here is what I do know. Jim Dunbar is from my district. He grew this airline on my watch. And this is a small town. Even Jim Dunbar doesn't understand how well I know his attorney and his banker." Orville paused and tilted his head. "So I know a little bit about your purchase contract."

So far, Orville's description followed the outline in Ripley's mind. But, not this far.

"Your holding company bought Jim Dunbar's airline, but you didn't pay him all his money. There was a holdback provision in the purchase agreement. Jim Dunbar wanted more money than Coriolis was willing to risk, so they negotiated an earn-out based on future passenger revenue. Pretty standard. I am not surprised.

"What I am about to suggest will boost your revenues outside of that agreement. Jim Dunbar won't get one thin dime. That means you come out a hero for Coriolis and we create a little rainy day fund."

The Ratchet

Al Ripley never cheated on his taxes. He always had solid backup for every deduction. He also never stole a freight train, but he knew the purpose of a rainy day fund. He already suspected that Hatchmeyer would propose a government subsidy to cover the shortfall, but he did not consider how it would be classified on his books. The government subsidy would not be booked as passenger revenue and so would be exempt from Jim Dunbar's earn-out. In the grand scheme of *total* airline revenue, Dunbar's payout was only a rounding error, but Al Ripley was a master at collecting rounding errors for personal gain. The bonus clause in his own executive contract would accrue enough dollars to keep Ripley interested.

The subtle smirk on his face betrayed his new understanding and gave Hatchmeyer all he needed to know about his new partner.

"Just one more thing," Orville raised his chin. "We need to bring in the union." He stopped to let the sentence sink in. Ripley was a player, but the game moved just beyond his balance point. Miniscule eye movements gave clear communication that he did not anticipate this move. "Your airline is coming up in the world," Orville continued. "It's time you started to play with the big boys."

Al Ripley was born at night, but not last night. He quickly put the pieces of this puzzle together. Orville filled in the gaps. "Your rainy day fund will most certainly fund your bonus, but you need to remember who made all this possible. So, here is the way this works.

"We bring in the union, organize your workers. You use what's left in your rainy day fund to increase wages on the front end and deduct their union dues off the back end. The union knows where to funnel their political contributions to make sure they stay in business. By the way, I expect a modest, and legal donation from the Ripley bonus pool. I have a campaign to run, my friend."

Hatchmeyer's eyes narrowed to see if he could ask for more. Ripley was stone faced, so Hatchmeyer continued to press. "You can pitch some cash to your management team. They can individually contribute to my campaign, as well. We'll have a little fundraiser, they can meet me. You tell them, it's all about access. Access to the system. Good for business."

Hatchmeyer made it sound easy. Ripley was not so sure. "You know, Mr. Hatchmeyer, Outbound never had a union. You make it sound like the workers will automatically vote to organize. It's a pretty independent bunch. I don't know if it will go that smooth."

"Now, Ripley. This is not your first time out of the barn. It's all about trust." Hatchmeyer smiled as he leaned forward and lowered his voice, again, that whisper voice. "Destroy the trust, they will organize. Take away a couple of holidays, stiff-arm their overtime, increase the deductible on their health insurance. They will organize. It's all about trust.

"I will send in some of my boys next week. You can hire them into your customer service department. Let them sow a few seeds. It won't be a problem, trust me."

The Tell

Like clockwork, four resumes hit Ripley's desktop the following Tuesday. Embedded in each resume was the *tell*. Extensive customer service experience, mostly invented, with just a sprinkling of community organizing. Ripley never spent much time reading resumes, and now was no exception. His finger hit the intercom. "Mindy, I am going to forward over a couple of resumes. Can you push them down to HR. Tell them I want to beef up our customer service department. Bring them on as interns. Pay them minimum wage."

There, it was done, the wheels in motion.

Until Wednesday, and a knock on the door. It was Mindy, swinging the door open wide. Behind her stood Outbound's director of HR, Marsha Feldman. Marsha moved quickly over to the chair directly in front of Ripley's desk. "Mr. Ripley, I got the resumes you sent down yesterday, and I am a bit confused. We spent a lot of time in personnel planning for all of our departments. Our customer service manager did a good job integrating our technology so our CSRs can cover all our customer channels, telephone, web site, email, chat and text. We have a personnel plan and we have bench strength both in scheduling our three shifts and in training. But, I have to tell you, these resumes looked good.

"It's funny, though. I thought I would give the candidates a call, standard screening. Normally, that screening would take a couple of days, but I got through to every one of them on the first ring. Anyway, just wanted to check. If we bring these people on, they are going to put us over on our personnel budgets. I know you said, bring them in at minimum wage, but, based on their resumes, they are going to want more money."

A hint of a smile came across Al Ripley's face. "Tell you what. You know how sensitive I am to budgets. Let's stick to minimum wage, see what happens. I think customer service is king, I want to beef up that department."

Play On

The following Monday was a bright sunshine day in Denver. Even Al Ripley had a keen appreciation for the crisp mountain air that cascaded down the foothills from the upper loft of the Rockies. This was a prelude to winter, a paradox of warmth piercing the dry cold of the atmosphere. The air put a spring in Ripley's step as he skipped across the parking lot.

Slipping in the back door to his office, he caught the light flashing on his telephone. Mindy heard the door close and popped in. "Mr. Hatchmeyer is on line one," she announced. "I don't think he is in a good mood."

Ripley waved her out, motioned for her to shut the door, as he put Hatchmeyer on speaker. "Al, are you playing games with me?" Orville was decidedly impatient.

"What's up?" Ripley replied.

"I told you to put my boys on the job, but I am getting complaints on my end and they haven't even started work there, yet. What is this minimum wage stuff? These boys are professionals."

It was Ripley's turn to agitate the other side. "Mr. Hatchmeyer, I thought you said it was all about trust. 'Destroy the trust,' you said. I'm just showing your boys how we play over here."

"Don't waste my time over this," Orville flatly stated. "There are other airlines who might be interested in some of your routes. Don't tempt me to call off this whole thing. I didn't get this far because I roll over. Either run this thing straight up or don't run it at all."

Over the phone, Orville Hatchmeyer could not see the grin on Al Ripley's face. His smile reflected a small victory, while his words placated Hatchmeyer's irritation. The two broke off the conversation with a fragile truce. Mistrust was in the air.

Crosswinds

Jim Dunbar told himself, "It's only an event. Just an event that has my attention." He stared at the 3x5 card on the bulletin board in the break room. As Chief Culture Officer, this was a smack in the face. "UNION MEETING, 7pm Tuesday night." How had he not known?

The issue of unionization was something Jim thought about as his airline grew up. Intuitively, he hated the thought that some outside organization could begin to dictate things on the inside. His management decisions, before the buy-out, were always well-balanced to consider safety, compensation and working conditions with profitability and risk.

Admittedly, in the beginning, the offices were small and some of the furniture was worn. But, compensation at all levels was competitive and Jim created a culture that made up for the lack of resources and lavish benefits.

But, now was different. Jim was no longer in control of his baby. The culture changed. As Chief Culture Officer, he began to feel helpless in the face of company initiatives that seemed to continually backfire. And now this, a union at the door. Jim had an uneasy feeling in the pit of his stomach.

Traction

Unions attempted to organize Outbound before, without success. Union reps visited to talk about higher wages, better health insurance, mandatory work breaks and limited work hours. In the past, what they found, at Outbound, were above market wages, gold plan health insurance and work conditions that created a waiting list to apply for the rare open position.

But this time was different. This time, the union was determined to penetrate. In spite of the reality of above market wages, the union gave speeches about substandard compensation. In spite of the gold plan health insurance, the union promised a better, union administered plan. They talked about a production slowdown for better working conditions. And this time, people began to take them seriously.

And there was valid concern. A new set of Ripley's Rules replaced the employee handbook. New oversight on overtime. All overtime to be reviewed, after the fact, by an overtime panel to determine its necessity. Unapproved overtime disallowed. Payment for approved overtime was delayed by two pay periods. Some of Ripley's Rules violated government guidelines, but were in force, nonetheless.

A new employee, on the job for less than three days, filed a harassment suit and his supervisor was placed on unpaid leave for a month. All vacation schedules were scrapped while an efficiency consultant conducted a study to create a more productive schedule with staggered days off. It appeared that Outbound cultivated an environment where trust began to deteriorate, as if mistrust was the objective.

Some of Ripley's Rules, when questioned, were reversed to something more sensible, at least in compliance with legal guidelines. Meeting after meeting sucked up managerial time with discussions about employee morale and covert back-stabbing. Then the inevitable rewrite of the Ripley Rule Book took even more administrative time.

And that's when the union got its hold. Most team members could see through the phony arguments that erupted, but they also felt helpless to fight back against the new environment of mistrust. The union was tearing the company apart. The team wanted to fight back, to restore the company they knew, the company they helped to grow.

There was a vote, an interesting vote. In the end it was a secret ballot, but prior to the secret ballot, there was plenty of public discussion. The union reps, now Outbound employees did their homework and propped up several egregious examples to influence the vote.

The union got traction.

Delayed Departure

The sunshine turned gray that morning. A gentle drift of snow began to fall as the small Outbound plane made a three-point landing in Dickinson. Ripley promised jet service to Orville Hatchmeyer's hometown, but, this touchdown was still a small passenger prop aircraft.

It was a short taxi to the terminal. There were two gates known as Fielder's Choice, for it never really mattered. Outbound Air was the only scheduled service and private planes always yielded. On this particular day, heavier and heavier flakes of snow obscured the taxiway from the runway. The lone figure at the gate stood like a dark ghost in a sea of white, waving orange cones to signal the arrival spot. In the space of three minutes after touchdown, visibility dropped to 50 yards.

Ground service personnel quickly joined the parking attendant, rushing to the aircraft door. They dragged the luggage cart through the squeaky snow underneath its frozen wheels. The pressure popped as the door released to drop a cascade of short stairs for passengers scurrying to grab their belongings. The track of pedestrians ignored the yellow lines on the tarmac now invisible beneath the white blanket.

It was supposed to be a quick turn. Passengers off, passengers on, safety briefing, taxi out and take-off. But the passenger destined for first class was late. Representative Hatchmeyer was still in transit to the airport in his black Chevy Suburban.

"Take your time," Orville admonished his driver.

"Yes, sir, but we are behind schedule, the plane is set to take off soon," his driver replied.

"Son, do you see this snow? That plane ain't going nowhere. And do you see me on board? That's two reasons the plane will be sitting at the gate waiting for us." Orville pulled out a short stub of cigar, then thought better of it. Why waste a good Cuban at this point. Even Orville Hatchmeyer could not smoke on the plane.

Rounding the chain link security fence between the parking lot and the terminal, Orville smiled. "See, what'd I tell you? The plane is still here. Going nowhere 'til I get on board. Mind my bags out of the trunk. And tip that fella well that loads 'em on the plane."

"Evening, Mr. Hatchmeyer," the TSA agent was cordial. "May I hold your coat for you while you go through security, sir?"

"Dang, blame security," Orville snorted.

"It won't be a problem, sir, but you have to step through the detector. And I wouldn't be in a hurry, looks like we are weathered in. We have snowplows on the runway."

Orville stood impatiently at the gate. Through the window, he could see the pilot in the cockpit. The gate agent offered a look of concern, displaying a sense of urgency in the face of a hopeless departure. More show for the benefit of Hatchmeyer, than an acknowledgement of reality. "Plane landed just before the wind blew that snowstorm in. Quite a build-up on the wings just sitting out there."

"If they're getting the snow off the runway, they better get that snow off the wings. I've got a dinner speech to give in Denver. Got to raise some campaign money, so you and your family can vote for me again." Orville peered over his glasses at the gate agent.

Overspray from the de-icer hit the window outside the gate. Water would have instantly crystallized on the glass, but the glycol solution gathered drops into rivulets, cascading down the window.

The gate agent smiled. "Yes, sir. As soon as that snow lets up, we will get you out of here. Looks like you're not traveling alone this afternoon."

It was not unusual for Hatchmeyer to be the only passenger, sometimes the plane even ran empty. But tonight, a newspaper reporter and a photographer joined him as traveling companions.

"Afternoon, Representative Hatchmeyer," spoke the cub reporter. "My name is Harry, Harry Richter. I cover environmental issues for the Times."

"The Times?" shrugged Hatchmeyer. "Which Times?"

"The Kansas City Times. Out here doing a story on the oil patch. Pretty sensitive stuff, you know. I understand you are heading to Denver to give a speech. Don't know if we are going to get out of here, today."

"Oh, we'll get out of here," Orville shook his head. "This is my airline, if I say we go, we go. I got the snow plows out there. We'll get out of here today, boys."

Harry turned to his photographer, to cover a roll of the eyes. "Yep, I have heard good things about this airline, ever since they were acquired by Coriolis. Is Dunbar still around?"

"Dunbar? Jim Dunbar? Only place you will see Jim Dunbar is in the history section of their website," Orville stared at the cub reporter. "Al Ripley is the one in charge, now."

Hatchmeyer's performance strut for Harry Richter was interrupted by a commotion in the cockpit of the plane outside the frosted window of the terminal. The pilot and co-pilot hung up their headsets. Two steps later, they emerged from the aircraft, proudly wearing their bomber jackets to ward off the elements as they scurried down the stairs.

The gate agent released the security door to whisk the two pilots inside. The wind caught the door as the two figures tumbled through the opening. Everyone looked at the door, pinned open in the wind, snow moving sideways onto the carpet.

"Somebody, get that door!" Hatchmeyer shouted. "Can't you see, it's snowing outside?" The gate agent ducked low and made a plunge into the wind, grabbed the door and slammed it shut.

"What's going on here?" Orville demanded.

"Sorry, Mr. Hatchmeyer," the co-pilot explained. "It looks like this storm is breaking up. If we could get wheels up in the next thirty minutes, we would be glad to fly you down to Denver. In fact, once we skirt this storm, it looks like a smooth ride."

"Then, what are you doing in here?" Hatchmeyer snapped. "The snowplows are on the runway. What are you boys waiting for?"

"You don't understand, Mr. Hatchmeyer. Our flight window expires in thirty two minutes."

"What do you mean, your flight window expires? Look, boys, I don't know what you are trying to pull here, but I have a speech to give in Denver. If you say that storm is breaking up, then I don't see what the problem is." As Hatchmeyer shouted, the pilot and co-pilot separated and began to walk in different directions. "You! You're the captain of this plane. What do you have to say for yourself?"

The pilot abruptly turned and calmly replied. "Mr. Hatchmeyer, in thirty-two minutes we turn into pumpkins. Union rules. We are only allowed a certain number of flight hours each day, each week. They are scraping the runway, but I just called in an overnight flight delay. We can take off in the morning."

Harry Richter may have been a cub reporter, but he had sufficient experience with politics to enjoy this repartee. He knew enough to stay out of the conversation, but he really could not help himself. He took a half step to get into Hatchmeyer's peripheral vision. Orville glanced over. Harry telegraphed an unspoken facial question. "I thought this was your airline. Are you going to let a pilot dictate a union rule?"

Orville bristled. "How long you been flying for this airline, son?"

The pilot took in a deep breath. He knew there was no right answer. "Fifteen years in the Air Force, thirteen years for Outbound."

Orville fixed his eyes. "If you don't get back in that airplane and get ready for take-off, then, today was your last day flying for Outbound."

The pilot smiled, nodded to his co-pilot and walked away.

Harry Richter moved his head to the side, to get a better view of a politician about to blow a gasket. Orville reached for his cellphone. The menu screen displayed a picture of Al Ripley. A fat thumb pressed on the picture and a radio wave raced through the snowstorm to the nearest cell tower and up to a satellite.

Al Ripley was in Washington DC, settling a bar tab. The productive afternoon turned dark as dusk settled in. A gentle vibration pressed against his side. As he drew the phone from its holster, he saw the pudgy face picture of Orville Hatchmeyer.

"Orville, I was just thinking about you," Ripley started with a smile. But the smile soon yielded to a scowl. "I understand," he replied. "Mr. Hatchmeyer, don't worry. I don't know if the storm is breaking, but if we can get the plane in the sky, we will get you down to Denver."

Ripley shook his head. "Yes, Mr. Hatchmeyer. You have my word. Yes, we know how much we owe our success to your efforts. We will get you down to Denver."

Sometimes, Al Ripley felt on top of the world. Sometimes, Al Ripley felt that being on top of the world, was a pain in the neck.

"Shit, Mindy, I don't care," Al blasted into the phone. "You have been my assistant for five years. You know whose strings to pull. This is just a flight from Dickinson to Denver. It's on our schedule. We have backup pilots somewhere. Get with flight operations and find somebody. If the weather clears, get Hatchmeyer down there, so he can make his goddamn speech."

Orville Hatchmeyer stood inside the gate with Harry Richter, his photographer and the gate agent, who tried to keep everyone calm. Orville made no secret about his phone call to Al Ripley. For him, it was all part of the performance.

The panes of glass in the terminal were now clear. The storm was breaking, snowfall light enough for a private plane to make an approach and a successful touchdown.

Orville turned to his new entourage. "You see, Harry, I told you we would get out to Denver tonight. I control this airline. If I say we go, we go."

The gate agent paced back and forth. "Mr. Hatchmeyer, good news. Yes, the weather is breaking, the runway is open, your plane was de-iced, but the best news is, we have a new pilot on his way over."

"Well, that is good news. We have just enough time to make it into Denver. I appreciate all your efforts this afternoon. This is very important to me."

The ticket agent hesitated. "I'm sorry, Mr. Hatchmeyer, you don't understand. The pilot is on his way, driving from Bismarck, but I am afraid it will be another forty-five minutes before he arrives."

"What? That is unacceptable. Is this the best this airline can do?"

"I am sorry, Mr. Hatchmeyer."

Race Against Time

Driving a borrowed pickup truck, Gordon Hill raced across the plains of North Dakota. Gordon liked fast things. Fast cars, fast motorcycles. In the winter, he raced snowmobiles. In the summer he rode bulls on the amateur rodeo circuit. He was a cowboy's cowboy. Machines and speed attracted him to flying.

Riding shotgun in the pickup was Louis Castillo. Louis always rode shotgun with Gordon. They went to high school together. They went in the military together. When Gordon entered flight training, he convinced Louis to tag along, said he needed a wingman. But, what came easy for Gordon was difficult for Louis. Without Gordon, Louis would have washed out.

Following an uneventful tour of duty, Gordon signed on with a small air cargo company. It took a few months, but he finally convinced the company to hire Louis. Together, they logged hours in the cockpit,

Gordon always the pilot in charge, Louis always right seat, as co-pilot. When they had enough hours, they applied to Outbound Air.

For eight months, Gordon flew only ferry flights, to re-position empty aircraft. Occasionally, he would get a slot as co-pilot on a passenger leg, but flying captain was a matter of seniority. He signed up for the union to make sure he got a fair shake, but even still, the competition for routes was tough. As a new pilot for Outbound Air, this might be Gordon Hill's big break.

When Gordon got the call, his first move was to phone Louis. His second move was to check the weather. The storm at Dickinson was lifting. He could tell, as he sped down the highway, that conditions were improving. The thermometer in the dashboard showed a temperature drop. Too cold to snow. The disappearing cloud cover allowed any earthbound heat to escape into the atmosphere. The moon appeared soft behind the haze, then crisp in the stark darkness.

Gordon knew people were waiting on him, important people were waiting on him. A state representative, a newspaper reporter and a photographer, all waiting on Gordon Hill. Heck, he could pull over and take a nap, they would still have to wait, because they were waiting on him. Today, Gordon Hill was a rock star.

Gordon walked tall into the terminal building. He showed his badge to TSA, who personally escorted him through security in the Fielder's Choice terminal.

"Boy, am I glad you are here," the gate agent whispered. "This guy is giving me the creeps. He acts like he owns this airline."

"Okay, okay, everything is under control. We're here, now," Gordon showed confidence. "A lot of snow today. I understand everything is plowed out. Plane de-iced?"

"Yes, the de-icing truck shot the plane and covered half the terminal, check the paperwork," the gate agent relayed. "The baggage is loaded, as soon as you give the all clear, we will get the passengers on board."

Orville Hatchmeyer interrupted the confidential whispers. "I don't want to break up this little party, son, but, I have a speech to give in Denver tonight. I called ahead and told them we would be late, but let's get this show on the road. Other planes are landing all around us, and we are still stuck on the ground."

"Yes, sir," Gordon smiled. "You can count on us." The two pilots trudged out to the plane, crunching through the snow.

"Get inside and make sure that heater is working," Gordon directed. His walk-around was brief as the temperature continued to plummet. His teeth chattered as he bolted up the stairs and settled in next to Louis. Two minutes later, the passengers followed.

Outside, the moon's reflection off the white snow almost gave the appearance of daylight. It was a brilliant, crisp night for flying.

Gordon sprinted through his checklist as flight operations released the flight. He looked down at his watch and picked up the radio.

"Yes, I am working out the de-icing time. You guys already hit us, but we're outside the hold-over window. We need to bring the truck back to give us another shot."

"10-4," came a crackled response. "But your plane was scheduled to sit here overnight. Our de-icer parked the truck and went home."

Gordon stared at his watch and pulled on the intercom. "Ladies and gentlemen, thank you for flying with Outbound. Looks like we have a small flight delay. The driver of our de-icing machine shut down for the day and we have to scare him up to give us one more shot before we get out of here. I will let you know, as soon as we find him."

Orville was in the midst of a short pre-flight nap when the announcement snapped him to attention. Unbuckled, he charged the cockpit door knocking once, then pounding twice. The flight attendant, caught off guard, rushed to the front.

"Mr. Hatchmeyer, Mr. Hatchmeyer, you can't knock on the door. FAA regulations say you have to stay in your seat. You can't be knocking on the pilot's door."

Orville whirled around, his face flushed red. "Young lady, do you know who I am? If you want to keep your job, you better get on the intercom and tell that pilot of yours that this flight cannot wait any longer. Other planes are landing. If your pilot thinks that some union rule is going to stop us from taking off, he has another think coming."

Gordon Hill heard the commotion outside the cockpit door. He glanced at Louis, but his attention was fixed in a conversation with the night assistant in airport maintenance. "Are you sure about the hold-over window on the de-icing fluid?" Gordon asked. "I know they use that stuff in Canada, but I didn't know we used it down in the States. Are you sure?"

The flight attendant stood staring at Orville. Orville stood staring at the flight attendant. Neither blinked.

The intercom rustled. Gordon Hill's voice was clear. "Ladies and gentlemen. Thank you for flying with Outbound Air, a Coriolis company. Kick the tires and light the fires. Flight attendant, please take your seat for an immediate departure."

Orville Hatchmeyer won. A smug smile crept over his face as he lumbered back to his seat. He closed his eyes as the engines accelerated and the aircraft rolled away from the gate.

Jim Dunbar had just finished dinner. Susan collected the plates and poured a cup of decaf coffee when Jim's phone pulsed an incoming call. He intended to let it go to voice-mail, but answered instead. Susan stopped to watch Jim fetch the remote control. The big TV in the living room glowed from dark to light. A news anchor described the scene over a live shot at the Dickinson airport, the Outbound logo in the corner of the screen. The next morning would reveal, straight off the runway, a thin stream of smoke, leftover from a small debris field. Something had gone terribly wrong.

Part Five

Human Error

The National Transportation Safety Board said they would conclude their investigation within six months. But, there was already rampant speculation. News channels interviewed on-air flight consultants and former pilots, unrestricted by investigation protocol.

It was unanimous, based on the circumstantial evidence. Pilot error was to blame. The de-icing window expired, yet for some unknown reason, the pilot forged ahead, pressing the envelope beyond the laws of nature and the technology of man.

A union representative was quick to comment, deploring work conditions at the airline. He accused Outbound of falsifying flight logs to cover up extended working hours of pilots. He questioned maintenance logs related to de-icing protocols and the purchase of sub-standard de-icing fluids.

Al Ripley refused to comment. His assistant Mindy expertly stiff-armed every request for an interview. Ripley issued a company-wide gag order. "Nobody talks," he screamed into his intercom.

Disciples at the Water Cooler

No one talked to the press. All media contact was frozen. Al Ripley was the only person with the authority to make a statement, and he followed his own advice.

But people talked in pairs by the water cooler. Conspiracy theories developed. Was it true? Was it false? And, who was to blame? Certainly someone was to blame.

Al Ripley, propped up by Coriolis, suddenly became the scapegoat. As the new CEO, he had promised all would be well, higher pay, benefits and union representation. His storyline threw Jim Dunbar under the bus. Al Ripley was the new savior. But all saviors eventually get crucified and it was Ripley's turn on the cross.

Fragging

Fragging is a military term to describe a chain of events where a trusted officer comes under scrutiny of his squad, for a promise broken. Originating in the Vietnam war, the story is about an officer who promised that if every team member followed orders, there would be a safe return to base camp. It was a promise that no officer could keep in a time of war. Inevitably, squad members would be wounded and killed, a promise broken, the squad betrayed by their commanding officer.

In due course, in the dead of night, a tent flap would be lifted, a fragmentation grenade rolled under the canopy of the sleeping officer and the wartime crucifixion would be complete. No savior survives.

Daniel Pursemeister was one of Ripley's supporters, but now under investigation into the purchase and fraudulent representation of substandard provisions, he turned. Under oath, Pursemeister rolled the grenade into the tent. He testified that he received an institutional directive that he purchase substandard goods, specifically orange de-icing fluid instead of green and that he was instructed to systematically falsify purchase orders and records to manage the cover-up. He produced payroll evidence that a portion of his compensation was converted to "incentive" pay. And that incentive effectively coerced him to falsify records to enhance the profitability of Outbound Air.

The Last Supper

Al Ripley's usual entourage gathered to wait out the verdict of the investigation. At times, one of them would disappear into a sequestered room to answer questions from an auditor. At this point, there were no criminal or civil charges pending, only speculation. Actual findings would not be known for months. But these speculations would alter the career of Al Ripley and the future of Outbound.

Maybe for the first time in his life, Ripley was nervous. He already emerged from a brief state of denial, thinking first, the news story of the crash was fabricated. Flipping from one news channel to the next, his denial quickly shifted from the reality of the tragedy to disowning any personal culpability. CEOs don't fly airplanes. How could anyone hold him accountable for this error in pilot judgment?

Yet, Ripley had a feeling in his stomach, somehow, this would be pinned on him. He received a short email from Samuel Pierce, Coriolis' chairman of the board, but then, communication went silent. No one called to ask how he was holding up to the NTSB investigation. Not a text, or a card, not even a note from his mother.

Stationed in the wings of the inner circle of the board was Ripley's sole supporter. Douglas MacBride was the head of the search committee to field CEOs for companies acquired by Coriolis. MacBride was instrumental in Ripley's appointment to run Outbound Air.

"Doug, how are things in the ivory tower?" Ripley's phone call began. "Just checking in to let you know everything is under control here in Denver."

There was a short silence on the other end. Douglas MacBride measured his response. "Al, you know I am a strong supporter for you. On the front lines, you make unpopular decisions, but at the end of the day, you make us a profit." He stopped. "But, you know, there have been times when you were unpopular with the rest of the board. But, I stood by you and some of your decisions."

Al Ripley knew the drill. "Get to it Doug. I know I placed this call to reassure you that everything is okay, but if you have some news I need to know, spill it."

"Al, what I am about to tell you is in strictest confidence. For the good of the airline and all the employees, this must not leak out until we are prepared. It's best for the company and it's best for you. If anyone finds out that I shared this with you, I will deny it. For the time being, I can protect you, as best I can. But if you tell anyone about this conversation, all bets are off and I can no longer shield your career from the inevitable."

When Ripley hung up the phone, he knew the churning in his stomach told the truth. His time with Outbound was numbered in days. The oath of confidentiality with his messenger, MacBride, prevented him from taking evasive action.

Worse yet, he knew Doug MacBride was no longer in his camp. MacBride, in his silence, would betray him to the board and the board would move to the next step unimpeded. His former friend became complicit in the death of his career. And Ripley silently consented.

The true causes of the crash would likely never be known. Only the superficial, isolated, description of pilot error. The organizational failures behind all the circumstances implicated not only Ripley's cunning and greed, but the board's incompetence to manage this rogue CEO with anything other than a bonus. This incident would end his career with Outbound, but Ripley's behavior would never be called to account and likewise, the board would never be called to account. Boards do not fly airplanes either.

Corporate Cake

The announcement came quickly, and caught everyone off guard, except for Al Ripley. A bright young man, named Kevin DuPont, with an MBA pedigree, would succeed Ripley as interim CEO, effective immediately.

Al Ripley was remanded to HR for a debrief. Marsha Feldman conducted many exit interviews, but this one was special. The hair on the back of her neck tingled as she realized that, for one brief moment, her agenda was more important that the CEOs agenda.

On the surface, she seemed contrite, apologizing to Ripley for having to conduct this unfortunate interview. It was a quiet interaction. With the apologizing and hand-wringing over, she was terse in her questions and he was brief in his responses.

There was an informal bon voyage, arranged by Ripley's assistant, Mindy. In the space of a week, Outbound Air lost a plane, gained a new CEO and baked a corporate cake for Al Ripley's departure. Mindy knew the corporate cake was meant for her as well. This was just another tour of duty.

Ripley's contract prohibited his termination for other than gross negligence or malicious intent to harm the company. So, for now, he was still on the team, just not in charge of Outbound. When he finally met with the board in Dallas, they told him as much.

"I tried, as best I could," Doug MacBride related. "But, you know how it is, ship goes down, captain gets fired. Doesn't make you a bad guy, but the board had to save face in the market. If we fire you, we still have to pay your contract for the next four years. So don't worry, we will keep you as part of the team. I am sure we will find you another assignment, sometime, soon."

The fix was complete, and Al Ripley would live to fight another day.

The New Savior

Kevin DuPont was a credentialed MBA. He read every reprint article ever published by the Harvard Business Review. Though his internal resume only listed experience running two Coriolis companies, the board thought he might be the perfect sacrificial lamb.

It was a strategy they perfected over a couple of decades. Occasionally a CEO in one of their portfolio companies would gaffe. It could be a sexual harassment suit, a product recall or an operational mis-step like Outbound. The board showed quick action by terminating the current CEO, knowing that where there is smoke, there is fire. The crucified CEO would be sequestered in contractual limbo out of the limelight, while an interim CEO would make the corporate apologies and promise swift resolution. But the board knew most of the fixes would be band-aids, and that, underneath the armor, the root-cause would live to fester another day.

Coriolis was a portfolio company, living on the spread between companies in their profitable upticks and jettisoned companies on the slide. A company like Outbound might have upward momentum in its future or might have reached its apex. Only time would tell. And Kevin DuPont would help them decide. He was groomed as an interim CEO, never to have a permanent assignment, but only to bridge the gap between the fatal flaws of an Al Ripley and the ultimate disposition of a company like Outbound Air.

This interim role, like the sacrificial oil in a car, accumulated all the dirt and poisons. And, as sure as the next service interval, the oil is drained and replaced, along with a new filter.

Kevin DuPont was not the new savior. Though he carried all the trappings, he was a placeholder.

Part Six

Off Campus

Even with Kevin DuPont's arrival, there was a temporary leadership vacuum. Wherever there is a void, something arrives to fill its space. The workforce at Outbound splintered into union factions, outside agitators and internal posers. The rumor mill was alive and well.

And that's how Peter, Frank and Johnny struck up a relationship with Jim Dunbar. During Al Ripley's tenure, Jim, as Chief Culture Officer was both directed and mis-directed. In Ripley's absence, Jim was free to engage in more candid conversations at all levels inside the company. In many ways, it was like Outbound in the early days.

Off campus, there was an Irish bar, Shamus O'Toole's Roadhouse Saloon, who owed its flourishing existence to Outbound employees. If one really wanted to know the internal workings at Outbound Air, O'Toole's held the pulse. It was also the gathering place where employees mourned the loss of an aircraft, a veteran flight attendant and two stand-by pilots. The mishap carried an anonymous quality but it was still deeply personal.

At O'Toole's, Jim Dunbar attended Outbound's version of a wake, where rumor and speculation dominated. There was victim talk about Outbound Air as the target of misfortune. The ambiguity of the future reared its head and the group was left to deal with the path going forward. What were the employees to think? Who was to blame? How were they supposed to react? What were they supposed to do?

Since Jim Dunbar was the former owner of Outbound, by practice, he rarely visited O'Toole's. Yet, between Al Ripley's departure and Kevin DuPont's arrival, he was the de-facto leader. None of Ripley's vice-presidents possessed the scant capability to cover the gap. Momentum kept most things moving, but there was this unavoidable vacuum of raw emotion and uncertainty.

And so, it was, that Jim Dunbar found himself standing at the bar, ordering a dark beer and listening to the banter.

"It's really tough to figure out where this company is going. But, things will get better as soon as DuPont gets here."

"It's a good thing this DuPont guy is showing up. I don't know how much longer we could have survived under Ripley. Something was bound to happen."

"You know what they say. All crumbs lead to the top. I am glad that son of a bitch got fired. Things will get back on track, as soon as DuPont arrives."

Jim knew he was not invisible, and the frankness struck him as odd. In less than a year, the company he built from scratch had come to this. The topics discussed at O'Toole's more clearly described Outbound's organizational challenges than any conference room planning session.

The Gang

The next afternoon, at 5:15, Jim found himself irresistibly drawn back to O'Toole's. In one sense, he was uncomfortable with the discussions at the bar, but at the same time, his discomfort let him know that those discussions were real. The description of the dysfunction at Outbound was candid, unedited and detailed.

There was complaining, for sure, lots of victim talk with stories to back it up. But there were three in the group who simply asked questions. Jim observed that the direction of the conversation was determined, not by the unfiltered stories, but by the questions that were asked.

The three who guided the conversation were Peter, Frank and Johnny. They remembered the good old days. Their tenure with Outbound Air tracked back to Jim Dunbar.

Peter handled one of the technical crews back then. Preventive maintenance was his game. "In aviation, you don't get a second chance," he would tell his team. "If your car breaks, you can pull over to the side of the road. If your boat breaks, at least you float. If an airplane breaks, in flight, all bets are off. For us, maintenance is life or death." For Peter, everything was by the book.

Frank was in charge of all flight crews outside of the cockpit. Flight attendants, gate agents and baggage handlers. "You are always in the public eye, and when you least expect it, you will be faced with..." he always paused for dramatic effect, "...a customer. You may think you are on the top end of the baggage conveyer in the belly of the plane and will never have to speak with a customer, solve a problem for a customer or make a decision about a customer. And then the zipper on a bag explodes. No, not the bag, just the zipper, but all their socks and underwear sit at your feet. You have a decision to make, and believe me, the customer will know what decision you made."

Johnny got to play with all the toys on the flight deck. The instrument panel used to be a non-glamorous collage of dials and switches. Now the cockpit was awash with flat panels and touch screens. "It's a video game on steroids," Johnny smiled. "Except that everything animated is real, and when dots touch, people die. We install electronic displays that your life depends on. If everything goes right, and most times, they do, we make the pilot's job look easy. It's when things go wrong, redundant systems become critical, warning lights pop and the right data streams to the pilot in an intuitive way so they can make the best decision."

All three were experienced, years in training, with unmatched enthusiasm. They loved their jobs. They had a cause, or rather, their cause had them.

But, even Peter, Frank and Johnny eventually supported the union. Against what they saw as corporate missteps, perhaps only the union could help right the ship. Outbound Air was the company they helped build and they wanted it back.

Culture Work

There was a knock on Jim Dunbar's door. The three stood outside, staring at the name placard. Jim Dunbar – Chief Culture Officer. The door swung open. "Come in, come in," Jim invited them to comfortable chairs around a small conference table. "Glad you guys stopped by to see me. What's up?"

Peter cleared his throat. "Mr. Dunbar, we know you overheard our discussion at O'Toole's, yesterday. We have come to talk with you about the morale in the company."

"Sounds ominous," Jim responded. "What did you have in mind?"

Peter held the floor, so he continued. "You know, we have been working here since *you* owned the company. Back in the early days, we could make sense of things. Maybe we didn't truly understand why things worked the way they did, but we had this intuitive sense that things were right."

"Go on," Jim prompted.

"We have been thinking about this company, and we're worried," Frank chimed in. "We just have some questions, and we think they are important."

"Well," Jim raised his eyebrows, "what are the questions?"

"It's all about morale, sir...and the union," Johnny replied. "Morale is bad. Everybody is complaining and afraid for their jobs. It didn't used to be that way."

"Easy to see that there is uneasiness. Aside from the obvious, what do you think is causing it?" Jim asked.

"We don't know what, but we do know when. It started when you sold the company."

The remark brought back brief pangs of guilt. "What do you think is different?" Jim probed.

"Let's start with compensation. Before you sold the company, we felt things were fair. We never thought much about what people got paid. But, then the union came in and they said wages were unfair. They talked about minimum wage, living wage, seniority, tenure, automatic raises. They talked about how it's tough to find good people, market scarcity for technical workers. They said the shortage in the labor pool should mean higher wages for everyone. During the union meeting it sounded logical, but as soon as the meeting was over, we couldn't make heads or tails of what they said.

"And, as we look around, we can't figure out why some people get paid more than other people. The things the union guys talk about don't make any sense."

"So, what's the question?" Jim pressed.

"You know," Johnny continued, "our technicians come to work every day, jump in their uniforms. They have projects to work on, with specific work instructions. During each shift, they follow safety bulletins and preventive maintenance schedules. And every week, they get paid a certain amount of money, less taxes, of course."

"And?" Jim nodded.

"And some of us are in supervisory roles. We create the schedules the technicians follow, make sure they have the right tools, equipment and supplies to do their work. Depending on what has to be done, we may authorize overtime or move our technicians around.

And every two weeks, we get paid a certain amount of money, less taxes, of course."

"So, what's the question?" Jim repeated.

"I'm getting to that. Because some of us are in manager roles, we look at work flows and analyze the best way to complete the projects on the schedule. We *monitor* work instructions and *improve* work instructions based on feedback from our technicians and supervisors. We look at the sequence of work and create systems that are efficient and predictable. And every month, we get paid a certain amount of money, less taxes, of course."

Jim just nodded.

"And here's the thing. Our supervisors get paid more than our technicians and our managers get paid more than our supervisors and we just wonder why? We think it has nothing to do with what those union guys are talking about, but we still don't have an answer."

Everyone stopped. Jim took out a piece of paper and wrote. "What is it, about a role, that makes it different from another role that determines a different level of compensation?" Jim read the words out loud. Peter, Frank and Johnny looked at each other, nodded in agreement.

Johnny picked it up from there. "You see, you might say it's all about experience. But Mary is one of our best managers, and I have to tell you. She doesn't know the back end of a torque wrench from a lug nut, but whenever she moves into a department, even a technical department, productivity goes up, turnover goes down and job satisfaction improves."

"So, you could say that Mary, as a manager, gets paid more, based on bottom line results," Peter explained. "But the first three months, her department's budget was in the red. The fourth month, it broke even. Took six months for her to turn it around."

Jim looked at the group. "So, it is still the same question. What is it, about a role, that makes it different from another role that determines a different level of compensation?"

"Oh, and that's just the first question," Frank whispered.

What's a Manager?

"There's more," Jim feigned surprise.

"Yes, there's more," Frank chuckled. "We think a company, at least one as complex as Outbound, cannot be run on some simple 'one minute' analogy. It might sound noble to make everyone *feel like an owner*. If they feel like an owner, they might make decisions like an owner. But I have worked for myself in a business before and I have worked for Outbound. The decisions are different, the problems are different. Heck, the decisions are different between our technicians and our supervisors, and different between our supervisors and our managers. The accountability is different."

Johnny was on the edge of his chair. "Think about decisions. With our technicians, their decisions mostly have to do with pace and quality. 'Am I working fast enough to get all of my work done in the time allotted?' and 'Does the quality of my work meet the specifications of the work instructions?' Pace and quality. Pace and quality. 'If I work faster, will that compromise the quality of my output?' and 'If I work slower to make sure the quality meets the spec, will I get all the work done that is scheduled for me to do?' Pace and quality."

"Here is one thing we do know," Peter chimed in. "We think everyone comes to work, at Outbound, every day, intending to do their best. We can watch a technician doing their best, yet, sometimes the output falls short. Maybe they couldn't finish an installation on time, or they have four maintenance items to do and the second item turns into a bag of worms, so they only finish three during their shift. Sometimes, in spite of doing their best, the expected output just doesn't get done. So, the technician gets called out and humiliated in front of the team, when the truth is, they were doing their best."

"But, isn't the technician accountable for all four items?" Jim asked.

"Of course," Peter continued. "But, here's the thing. Let's say the technician couldn't finish a project because the shop runs out of materials. Or a specialized piece of equipment isn't available, or it takes two people and no one else is around to help. There is someone in charge of all those things, but it's not the technician, it's his manager. We are wondering, if the technician is accountable for doing his best, is it the manager who is accountable for the output of the technician? It's the manager who controls all the variables around the technician – supplies, equipment, tools and other personnel. Should it be the manager who is accountable for the output of the technician?"

"And, if the technician simply does not know how to do the work?" Jim asked.

"It's the manager who picked the technician in the first place and gave him the work to do. It's the manager who determines what training happens before the work is assigned. It's the manager who is accountable."

"Aren't you just trying to let the technician off the hook?" Jim wanted to know.

"Not at all," Johnny jumped back in. "We think there are some things the technician is accountable for – like a contract." Johnny hopped to an empty white board and began to write.

Team Member Contract[iii]
- Come to work every day and do my best.
- If, while doing my best, I get behind and cannot complete all my work, I have to let my manager know, ASAP. (Pace)

- If, while doing my best, I get ahead of schedule and have time to complete additional work, I have to let my manager know, ASAP. (Pace)
- If, while doing my best, my work does not meet the quality standard, I have to let my manager know, ASAP. (Quality)
- If, while doing my best, my work exceeds the quality standard, I have to let my manager know, ASAP. (Quality)
- If I am unable to do my best, because I don't feel well or some circumstance prevents me from doing my best, I have to let my manager know, ASAP.

"You see," Johnny continued, "the manager controls all the resources. The technician is accountable for doing their best, but it is the manager who is accountable for the output."

Why?

"Okay," Jim interrupted. "I am writing down your questions and your observations, but I have to ask why? Why are the answers important?"

Frank sat up straight. "You know, when that airplane went down and Ripley got sacked, it made us think. What are we doing here? Everything looked so prim and proper. All the vice-presidents wore neckties, we had policies and procedures, we even had an HR department. But it still didn't feel right.

"It felt different from when you owned the company. You never talked about how or why you ran things the way you did, but you must have had an instinct for what was right. We just thought it would be helpful.

Maybe we could get back to the old days, if we could just figure a few things out."

So, the commiseration at O'Toole's migrated inside the walls of the company. Three supervisors asked questions about how and why people work. The answers were elusive.

Commander in Chief

Kevin DuPont settled into his role as the new CEO at Outbound Air. He instinctively knew he was chum for the circling sharks. There were outside investigators, internal auditors, union activists coupled with uncertain morale. But chum was his role. He didn't actually have to clean up the mess, just outlast the panic. And he was smooth. In public, he could read from a teleprompter, canned messages created by an outside team of public relations specialists. He looked good in a suit. The angle of his jaw gave off a certain decisiveness, disarming skeptics and deflecting criticism.

Kevin calculated his tenure at Outbound Air would be about six months. At that point, the press and the public would forget the crash in Dickinson. The NTSB investigation would wrap up with a report about pilot error. And Kevin DuPont would be sent to another company in the portfolio going through a transition.

Kevin sat at Al Ripley's former desk, wondering how to occupy his time. His instructions from the board were firm. "Give the appearance that we are fixing things and don't piss anybody off."

Discovery

It wasn't late, but Jim was tired from the day. Television was an occasional diversion. Susan retired for the evening, in retreat to the bedroom. There was a sharp rap on the front door.

Jim went alert. He seldom had visitors this time of day. Startled. The sharp rap on the door yielded to muffled thuds, a different knocker, so Jim knew he had two visitors. As he struggled from the comfort of his favorite chair, the ruckus on the front porch subsided. No sound at all. Finally, the soft chime of the doorbell politely announced there were definitely guests who needed attention.

Jim peered through the security eye to verify his callers were friendly. He swung the door wide. "It's late," he observed. "What's up guys?"

It was Jim's Culture Club, Peter, Frank and Johnny. A bit animated, it never occurred to them that the hour was late or that their news could wait until tomorrow. Jim shook his head and chuckled. "You guys have been drinking, haven't you?"

The three looked at each other, realizing their stopover might have been at an inappropriate hour. "Ah, yes," Peter took up the explanation. "We were down at the pub having a pint, and we think we found it."

"Found what?" Jim wanted to know.

"Could we come in? It's kind of important. And we're not sure we can explain it, tomorrow. Can you help us put it together, tonight?"

Jim had no idea why he allowed the group access to his living room, but he was curious. "Can I get you guys some coffee?" Jim asked.

"No, no, no," Peter continued. "We promise this won't take long, we just need to put these pieces together. In fifteen minutes, we will know if we are on the right track. We can figure out the rest tomorrow down at the shop."

"All right, boys. Sit down, let's hear what you have to say," Jim was being polite.

It was Johnny who picked up the discussion. "Doc, you know we have been talking for the past couple of weeks about the work back at the plant?"

Now, Jim Dunbar was educated, but never close to a degree or a certification that would have prompted someone to believe he was a doctor, neither a doctor of medicine nor a doctor of philosophy, but Johnny always called him Doc.

"Well, yes," Jim nodded.

"And we have been talking about the difference in the work the technicians do and the work the supervisors do? And the difference in the work the supervisors do and the work the managers do?"

"Gentlemen, we have been talking about this for a couple of weeks," Jim said. "And our discussions have been orderly. Why the sudden urgency to barge in here tonight? Are you sure you only had a pint?"

"Doc, could it have anything to do with time?"

"Could what have anything to do with time? You will have to forgive me, but I am not following this." Jim still had patience for the conversation, but only if there was a significant point to be discovered.

Frank jumped in next. "There is a difference in the work that the technicians do," he tried to explain. "You know we tried to figure out why the engineering supervisor gets paid more than the technician out on the floor. We thought maybe it was experience, but we've got technicians with way more seniority than some of our supervisors. We thought it was skill, but there is no way the engineering supervisor could operate some of the machinery we have on the floor. So, if it's not skill and it's not experience, what is it?" Frank stopped. He might have stopped for dramatic effect, but, truth be told, he stopped because he did not know the answer to his own question.

"Doc, could it have anything to do with time?" Johnny repeated.

So, the Culture Club indeed stumbled onto something, but the idea was not completely formed. So unclear was their discovery that by tomorrow, the opportunity to understand it would be gone. That was their urgency to disturb the peaceful evening in Jim Dunbar's living room.

"Tell me more," Jim invited.

"Well, you know the technicians, they get paid by the hour. And the engineering supervisor, why, he gets paid by the week. And the managers' compensation is stated, by the month. And the Vice-Presidents, their compensation is stated on an annual basis. Could the difference in the work they do, have anything to do with time?"

There was a stunned silence in the room. The Culture Club spilled their guts. Over a pint, they stumbled on to this idea, but it would be up to Jim to parse it out, to see if the idea had legs.

"It's not just the pay," Peter followed on. "If you look at what the technicians do, everything is organized around their work day. They get their work instructions in the morning, and at the end of their shift, they put all their tools away. And look at the supervisors. We have to look ahead and create the schedules. We have to make sure supplies are ordered and that the equipment is in working order and available for specific projects. And the managers, their work is different too. They constantly walk the floor, looking at the sequence of the work, looking for ways to be more efficient. They have to turn in annual budgets and go to planning meetings. Could the real difference between the work the technicians do, the work the supervisors do and the work the managers do, have anything to do with time?"

The conversation paused once again. This *was* a different way of looking at the work in each of the roles they described. Jim moved to the kitchen to find a piece of paper. A napkin might have been more appropriate to record the elements of their conversation, but a notepad beside the refrigerator rendered a more suitable surface. They talked for a few more minutes, then Jim adjourned the meeting.

"Home, go home, not back to the pub. This is interesting. I will see you guys tomorrow morning, half hour early, in the break room."

The Culture Club completed their obligation to deliver the idea to Jim. Their discovery in the pub that night might truly be the missing link, to understand work, to understand levels of work and the capability required to be effective in each level.

"What was that all about," Susan asked, as Jim's head hit the pillow.

"Oh, some of the guys I work with are stumped on a project. They may have a breakthrough," he replied.

"It couldn't wait until tomorrow?" Susan asked.

"Apparently not," Jim closed his eyes, reconstructing the picture he drew on the notepad. "Apparently not."

Does It Have Anything To Do With Time?

"Okay, I am looking at my notes from the first time you showed up at my office," Jim started. "Here was your question. What is it that makes one role different from another role? So different, the company pays it out differently, one role to the next? And last night, you guys came by my house, you wanted to know if the answer had anything to do with time?"

Peter, Frank and Johnny looked at each other and nodded in agreement.

"And whenever we get together," Jim continued, "you consistently describe the work at three levels. Technician, supervisor and manager. You are very clear as you talk about the accountability in each role. So, let's just focus on that."

It was Peter who spoke next. "If we connect time with the job, does that get us anywhere?" he asked. "Why don't we start at the technician level?"

Frank jumped in. "So, the technicians that work on our airplanes, they come to work every day. They get instructions from their supervisors. Jim, I remember, when you ran Outbound, we had a huddle meeting every morning. It was quick, no chairs because we didn't have time to sit down. The supervisor laid out the work for the day, including projects from the day before that were not finished. Sometimes, overnight, things changed, priorities on one aircraft switched to another aircraft. But the goal for the day was always clear."

"Think about time," Jim said. "I'm going to write this down on the white board."

"That's it!" Johnny yelled.

"What's it?" Jim asked.

"The goal for the day was always clear," Johnny's speech quickened. "What's a goal?"

Everyone in the room looked at each other. They all knew what a goal was, but they didn't know the answer to Johnny's question.

"Look," he continued, "what's a goal? When you break it down, there are only two pieces to a goal. It's a WHAT, BY WHEN. Funny, whenever we think about goals, we always focus on the WHAT part, but guess what? Maybe, it's the BY WHEN that connects to time."

There was still confusion in the room. Even Johnny wasn't sure what he just said.

"Can you say that again?" Jim asked, watching Johnny's eyes go deep inside, trying to recreate the thought.

"A technician has a goal, given to him by his supervisor," Johnny recited. "There are certain WHATs that have to be completed. BY WHEN? By the end of the shift. The time span of the task is one day," Johnny thought he was being clear.

Frank looked at him sideways. "But how is that different for the supervisor? He needs the plane finished in one day, too."

"Yes, but the technician is only thinking about that one plane on that one day. The supervisor probably has five planes going in various stages of tear-down and maintenance. Plus he is ordering all the supplies, watching the tools and scheduling the technicians. The supervisor, to be effective, has to look ahead."

"How far ahead?" Jim asked.

Johnny was puzzled, but he wasn't stumped. "Well, it is certainly more than one day."

"Well, you said this all tied back to the BY WHEN of the goal," Jim prompted. "What is the supervisor's goal?" He stopped. "And I am not talking about the everyday goals. What's the biggest goal?"

Johnny was on a roll. "I can talk from personal experience. This airline has grown, so we're not a small fleet anymore. We get maintenance bulletins in all the time. I go over these bulletins with my manager and we make scheduling decisions a year out for all the aircraft. My manager is responsible for the whole fleet, but I control the workflow on the floor. We don't fix a plane when it breaks. We have to fix a plane *before* it breaks. So we have preventive maintenance schedules for all the planes coordinated throughout the year, twelve months' time span. Obviously, short term repairs come along, but, if we don't schedule out the long term maintenance, we can never work in all the short term stuff. Things can get pretty fluid, at times, easy to get in the weeds.

"One thing my manager always tells me. The company makes a lot more money when the airplane is in the air than when it's in the shop. That is why scheduling is so important. Prior to a scheduled maintenance turn, we may focus really hard for a couple of weeks, just to make sure the plane gets in and out in one day." Johnny sat back in chair.

"Okay," Jim took over the pause. "We have two data points. We have a technician and a data point at one day, and a supervisor with a data point at one year." He glanced at the clock. An hour elapsed and they only had two dots on the white board. "Let's call this meeting over. You boys have other work to do. But, say, you mentioned one of our managers, Mary. You said she did a pretty good job even though she doesn't know one end of the torque wrench from another. Why don't you fellows invite her to our next meeting?"

"When's that?" Peter asked.

"This is your meeting, you decide," Jim replied.

Roles

When Jim walked into the meeting room, he was surprised that someone commandeered his white board. When he left the day before, there were two dots, now there were nine. Someone drew horizontal lines across the board, and numbered each level. Three dots in each level.

III	Manager	O O O
II	Supervisor	O O O
I	Technician	O O O

"What's this?" he asked.

Peter, Frank, Johnny and Mary turned around. Mary was the first to speak. "Hi, Jim. I want to thank you for inviting me to join this group. The guys have me up to speed."

"Looks like you have taken what we started and moved it along," Jim said and sat down at the back of the group, leaving Mary standing at the white board.

"When I got here," she started, "it looked like you defined the time span for a technician role at one day and the time span for a supervisor role at one year. But, the reality is, even in a technician role, there are longer time span goals than one day. In fact, the observable work they do, turning wrenches and replacing parts, may be the shortest of their goals. You have heard the joke, ten seconds to turn the lug nut, ten years to know *which* lug nut. We send our technicians to school all the time for certifications on specific aircraft. Even a veteran technician, pushing a new certification, may take three months to learn the systems and reach an entry level of competence on that aircraft."

Mary stopped to make sure everyone followed her thinking. "So, in this range, for a technician, I have added dots going up to three months."

			Time Span
III	Manager	O	
		O	
		O	
II	Supervisor	O	
		O	
		O	
I	Technician	O	-3 months
		O	
		O	-1 day

"Same thing with supervisors," she added. "Occasionally, we find one of our lead technicians with the potential to become a supervisor. We have to be very careful with this, because a great lead technician does not necessarily make a good supervisor. Not only is it a different skill set, but there is a certain level of maturity involved. Sometimes, I think a person has to grow into the role."

Again, Mary stopped. She wanted to make sure everyone kept up. "So, when we test someone for potential," she started slowly.

"Wait," Jim interrupted her. "How do you test someone for potential?"

"Only one way I know of," Mary smiled. "I give them a project to do."

Jim chuckled. He was glad this was not some new psycho-profile assessment. Mary's method was pure managerial work, no tricks.

"Now, the project work has to contain elements of what a supervisor does," Mary continued. "It has to contain a supervisor level problem and a supervisor level decision."

"I got it," Peter piped up. "When I look at my crew, I always try to spot the person who can step up, take over for a bit when I have to leave the floor, go to a meeting. Sometimes, I test them with a project. Like, can the crew member create a personnel and equipment schedule for a week ahead?"

"And, what if they screw it up?" Frank asked.

"So, what?" Peter replied. "If they screw up a little project, it's no big deal."

"But, if they don't screw up the project," Mary guided things back, "we give them more project work, and more project work until we are certain they can competently perform at a higher level. Even then, they are still an entry level supervisor. In no way can they think out a year, but they can certainly handle things out to three months."

Properties in Level of work		
Level of Work	Typical Role	Longest Time Span Goal
III	Manager	
II	Supervisor	
I	Production Technician	1 day to 3 months

"Okay, stop," Jim jumped in. "The purpose of this discussion is to figure out if the difference between roles has anything to do with time. We may have stumbled onto a workable framework, but, in what way can we best define the importance of time span related to the work?"

Mary still had the floor. "Time span is the length of time that a person can effectively work into the future, using their own discretionary judgment, to achieve a specific goal."

Utter silence filled the room. Mary's pronouncement stopped the conversation. Jim scribbled the definition on a white board.

Peter glanced at his watch. "I agree, but we also have to get some other work done around here. I gotta bug out of this meeting. There's a team huddle that I need to be in."

Management by Walking Around

As Kevin DuPont walked the halls, he admired the teamwork posters on the wall. "Good idea," he thought. "From the outside, this place looked like a warm and fuzzy family."

"Jim Dunbar," Kevin announced his entry. "Chief Culture Officer. I like that."

Jim looked up from his desk. "Hi, you must be Kevin DuPont," Jim stood up. "Welcome to Outbound Air."

"Thank you. Thank you. I understand you built this airline from scratch? Quite an accomplishment. This is my third assignment in the Coriolis portfolio. It's no small accomplishment to get on their radar, much less to be acquired. I'm impressed."

Jim took it in. Kevin DuPont was certainly different from Al Ripley.

"Well, this is not quite the same airline that I sold to Coriolis," Jim acknowledged. "Bigger fleet, more gates, larger footprint. Without Coriolis and their investment, I could never have grown this big, this fast."

"I know. That's why I climbed on board Coriolis when I got my MBA. Nothing like the fast track." Kevin stopped. There was an awkward pause. Jim Dunbar was used to reading between the lines of Al Ripley. He was not certain how much trust to place in Kevin DuPont.

"I never heard of a Chief Culture Officer," Kevin smiled. "I know you are just working here through your earn-out. Honestly, most of the CEOs who sell to Coriolis and get paired up with Al Ripley quit within three months. It usually costs them a pretty penny, but they leave anyway. Who came up with Chief Culture Officer?"

It was Jim's turn to smile. "Ripley's idea. I think he tried to be funny, but after a while, I warmed up to the role. Before I sold the company, I think it was culture that created our success."

Kevin DuPont was all ears. He had read a hundred articles in the Harvard Business Review on culture. "Yes, I can see that. All the teamwork posters on the wall, really makes a difference."

Jim's smile turned into a short chuckle. "Nah, those were Ripley's teamwork posters. Don't read too much into them."

"Really? I think they're a nice touch," Kevin responded. "We are going to leave them up, aren't we?"

"You're the CEO," Jim explained. "Your decision."

"But you are Chief Culture Officer, and I think teamwork is part of a good company culture. Besides, as the new CEO, I think you will find me a pretty democratic guy. I think the best decisions are group decisions. I really trust my people. I think together we can decide."

Jim raised his head slightly. "For now, let's leave them."

"Good decision," Kevin applauded. "You know, I would like to bring that same kind of decision making to the rest of the team. I've known Al Ripley for quite some time. He can be a little autocratic and it's likely everyone needs a little change of pace here."

"Interesting," Jim observed. "How do you plan to make that change of pace?"

"Oh, we'll start at the top. At first, it will be subtle, but I think morale will improve when everyone gets a chance to participate. I want to begin with my executive management team. In fact, we have a meeting scheduled for tomorrow morning and I would like you to sit in."

Jim searched his mental calendar. The executive team meeting would interfere with Culture Club. He might have to delay their next meeting.

Changing of the Guard

Jim showed up thirty minutes early. He remembered his first executive team meeting with Ripley. He took a chair in the back of the room. As people filtered in, Jim could call them by name, but he could never tell them apart. The same starched white shirt and rep tie, button down collars.

Kevin DuPont arrived five minutes early. He had a written agenda with copies for everyone. "Welcome," he began, introducing himself with a summary on his background. "Over the next few weeks, I want to get to know all you, better. I've worked with Coriolis for some time. This is my third tour with them. I will be upfront with you. They only send me in when there is trouble.

"You also knew my predecessor, Al Ripley. He ran things by the book, command and control. I think you will find my management style a bit more refreshing. I think a team approach is important to the success of any company, so from now on, please think of yourself as a team. We will work as a team, make decisions as a team and solve problems as a team. We will succeed as a team or we will go down as a team."

Jim listened. He wanted to give the new guy a chance.

Back at the Shop

The Culture Club now numbered four. Peter, Frank, Johnny and Mary were hard at work while Jim met with the executive team. The framework on the white board accumulated more detail. They parsed through the roles at each level, fixed on a single idea. In the role, what was the longest time span goal? Not the average time span goal, not the median, what was the longest time span goal?

Properties in Level of work		
Level of Work	Typical Role	Longest Time Span Goal
III	Manager	12-24 months
II	Supervisor	3-12 months
I	Production Technician	1 Day to 3 Months

Peter pressed Mary for details at the manager level.

"When I first became a manager," she explained, "I had to create an annual budget. I had to think out for twelve months and, based on the company's targets, I had to imagine what kind of staff I would need, what my consumables would be and what my capital budgets would be. My first year, as a manager, I misjudged things by a mile. My second year, the company grew 20 percent ahead of plan, so my budget was still off. That was when I learned that, not only did I have to create a

121

plan, I had to create contingency plans, one for unusual growth and one for unusual contraction. I kept complaining those things were outside of my control and my manager just laughed and welcomed me to the world of management.

"Third year, my estimates were much closer, but my capital budgets didn't get approved. All the other managers got theirs approved, so I was stumped, chalked it up to inexperience. That's when I found out it had nothing to do with experience.

"The reason the other manager's got their capital budgets approved was because they looked two years ahead. The stuff that got approved this year got turned down last year. To be more effective in my capital planning, I had to think two years out. And not just put a plan together with the words *Two Years* at the top, I had to execute to that plan.

"Only the essentials of my capital budget would get approved each year, so I had to make do. The next year, most of the carry-over stuff would finally be approved, as long as it was necessary."

Democratic Decision Making

As time ticked by, Kevin DuPont's democratic decision-making began to show some cracks. The executive management team got together each week to kick around the most pressing issues. But Kevin and his team were often at loggerheads when it came around to budget issues. Each department seemed to have its favorite projects.

The starched white shirts would gather in pairs, making deals on the side to support this budget item or that odd project. As presentations were made, the team was slow to poke holes, for fear their pet project would be subject to the same scrutiny.

The *Executive Team Meeting*, it was called. There were hidden agendas, under the table handshakes and unconscious agreements not to spoil the day for each other. Each meeting's agenda was like a stepping stone across a creek. Quick strides for each measured step. If a stepping stone was unstable, discussion moved quickly to the next item. Real problems in the agenda were avoided. There was collusion, not cooperation. There was defensiveness, not inquiry. This was the *Executive Team Meeting*.

But, as the budget dollars piled up, Kevin DuPont could smell trouble. "Look, guys and gals, boys and girls. I know you all have important projects, but all this costs money. And you know very well, I am accountable to the board to make sure this company is fiscally sound. I am afraid that I have to take issue with the budget you have presented."

There was silence in the room. After all, the executive team just followed instructions. They followed Al Ripley's instructions, before. They followed Kevin DuPont's instructions, now. Finally, one person had the courage to speak, Javier Ramirez.

"Mr. DuPont, with all due respect. We are only doing what you told us to do. You said you empowered us with group decision making. Give us a problem to solve and leave it to us.

"Well, we decided on a budget, and I know that the expenses are more than our current revenue, but if we are going to grow, we have to take risks. The group is willing to take that risk, but now, you are pulling the rug from underneath us."

Kevin turned a red tinge around the rim of his ears, his pulse quickened. "That was not my intention. I want each of you to feel better about being a part of this management team. That is why I empowered you. But I also know my board and they will not stand for another losing quarter. The plane we crashed put a dent in our passenger counts. The government is auditing the subsidies on some of our routes. This airline has to learn to stand on its own."

"But, you said you trusted us, it would be our decision," Javier stood up. "It is a matter of empowerment."

"I know, I know," Kevin continued to defend. "But I am accountable to the board. If we lose money next quarter, you will all still have your jobs. You are not accountable to the board. It's me whose job is on the line. You are only accountable for the performance of your departments. All I can say, at this point is, I'm sorry. Meeting adjourned."

The starched shirts filed out of the room. There was no grumbling, no hostility and no defiance. For all Kevin DuPont tried to accomplish with democratic decision making, the uncertain state of morale at the top was unchanged. And morale at the top, even unspoken, had an impact on morale throughout the enterprise.

Accountability and Authority

When Jim was available, the Culture Club met. When Jim was not available, the Culture Club met. As a group they would not be deterred.

"I think we have these roles sorted out," Peter proclaimed. "I like the picture. It makes sense. But how do these roles relate to each other? I mean, who decides *who* is whose manager?"

Johnny jumped in. "It's true. Whenever someone new joins the company, that's always the first question. Who will this new person report to?"

Jim Dunbar knocked gently on the door. "Hope I'm not disturbing. How are things going?"

"We have a problem," Johnny declared. "Who decides who reports to whom? Whenever we have a new employee, we all sit around the table and that's the question. Who will this new person report to?"

Mary looked out the window, but suddenly turned and came back into the conversation. "Usually, we unload the new guy on the manager or supervisor who is the least busy."

"Is that the best way to do it," Jim asked.

Mary kept rolling. "Not a chance. Our supervisors are always busy, so sometimes the new technician reports to me. I have to tell you, I am a team player, but dealing with technicians is sometimes tedious and I lose my patience."

"Besides, Mary, no offense," Peter chimed in, "but you're not very technical anyway."

Frank took over the confrontation. "Could it have anything to do with time?" he asked. "Time helped us understand levels of work. Could levels of work help us understand who reports to whom?"

"You are talking as if this company was a military organization," Jim interrupted. "What if it has nothing to do with reporting? Think about it. When we work around here, we report to lots of people for all kinds of things. Technicians may report to one crew chief for a job one day, and report to someone else on a special project the next day. Everybody reports to lots of people, even in other parts of the company. What if it had nothing to do with reporting?"

"If we don't use the word *report* to describe the relationship between the technician and the supervisor, how do we describe it?" Frank looked for clarification.

"When the supervisor and the technician get together during the day, what do they talk about?" Jim asked.

Johnny jumped in. "When I talk to my team members, we talk about the work. We talk about decisions to make and problems to solve. We talk about the day's goal, the objective and the output. We talk about accountability."

"Whose goal is it?" Jim wanted to know. "I thought you said that you expected your technician to show up and do their best. So, whose goal is it? Who is accountable for the output of the technician?"

Mary was thunderstruck. "You're right, it has nothing to do with the technician reporting to the supervisor. It's about accountability. And the supervisor is accountable for the output of the team. When we have a new team member, it's not a question of who should the team member report to. It's a question of which manager, or supervisor will be accountable for their output."

"And that's the person who should be their manager," Peter concluded.

Johnny circled back to Mary. "So why is it tedious for you to be the manager of a new technician?"

"It's not that I can't be bothered by the decisions and problems of a technician, it's just that I feel like I am dragged into the weeds," Mary explained. "I am focused on a $250,000 budget item and the technician wants to know which torque setting to use. To the technician, it is a meaningful question related to the quality of the work output. For me, it is a detail that pushes me out of strategic issues and pulls me into tactical issues."

"I know what you mean," Johnny replied. "As a supervisor, I am much more interested in what the technicians do, because their work directly relates to my objectives. I live halfway in the weeds every day, it's part of my role."

"Does it make sense, then, no matter the role, that person's manager should be in a role one level of work above?" Peter thought out loud.

"Yes," Mary agreed. "Two levels of work is too far, one level of work feels about right."

Johnny was not finished poking holes in the discussion. "But what about having a manager in the same level of work?"

"God, no," Mary yelped. "That's all I need, someone at my level of work breathing down my neck. Their decision making is no better than mine. Their problem solving is no better than mine. If I am in trouble, with a tough decision or a tough problem, I want someone who can bring value to that decision, and it's certainly not going to be anyone at my level of work."

Jim looked at the emerging pattern. "So, to be an effective manager, may require that person to be competent in a role, one level of work above. With that capability, the manager can bring value to the problem solving and decision making of the team, one level of work below."

Properties in Level of work		
Level of Work	Typical Role	Longest Time Span Goal
III	Manager	12-24 months
II	Supervisor	3-12 months
I	Production Technician	1 Day to 3 Months

"So, hierarchy has nothing to do with reporting to each other," Mary said. "It has everything to do with creating this value stream, where managers bring value to the problem solving and decision making of their teams. And we can measure all this by looking at the longest time span goal in each role at each level of work."

But Doesn't This Look Like a Hierarchy

"You know, this is beginning to look like a hierarchy," Johnny said. "Do you remember Preston Pratney? If there is one thing he railed about, it's that hierarchy is bad. It goes against all the tenants of *Tribal Leadership*. Having layers inside the company makes it too bureaucratic, too much red tape. If there is a decision to be made, why should someone have to check with their manager?"

Mary stepped in. "You're talking about Preston Pratney? The problem with Preston is that he read too many books on leadership. He never understood the purpose of hierarchy. He got it confused with command and control. Hierarchy is necessary, to create this value stream for decision making and problem solving."

The Executive Team Meeting

Kevin remained perplexed. He was certain that democratic decision making would turn morale around. But now, he could feel the quiet whispers behind his back.

"What are you thinking about?" Jim asked, poking his head in Kevin's door, something he could never imagine when Al Ripley was CEO.

"The *Executive Team Meeting*," Kevin shook his head. "You know, it's really a pretty good team, but I could see the disappointment in their faces when I didn't go along with their decision. Kind of like I let the air out of their balloon."

"So, what can we learn from this?" Jim pressed.

"I don't know," Kevin pursed his lips. "Even in the run-up to the last meeting, I could see something wasn't right. I told the executive team that they would have a lot of latitude, but it seemed to turn them into a bunch of power-brokers. I could see the clandestine handshakes, under the table deals to support a pet project here and there. I wanted them to come together, but it seeded competition and friction."

"When you step back and analyze what is happening in the *Executive Team Meeting*, what do you see?" Jim asked.

"Sometimes, the meetings are totally irrational, they don't make sense. The people in the seats sound like different drummers, out of sequence, off rhythm.

Whenever we look at a problem, minds are already made up. We rarely dig deep enough to make an informed decision. I mean, look at the budget they came up with. Sure, it would be nice, but the income statement would be under water, no basis in reality.

"And some of the quid pro quo in there. The support for one project or another has nothing to do with the merits of the project. Team members are pairing up and making deals with each other at the water cooler.

"They are out of control, and I don't know how to reign it back in. I know they are complaining about me behind my back. It's like they aren't even thinking."

Jim drew on his notepad. Some of it looked like genuine doodle, but in the margin, he sketched a comparison chart.

Not in work mode[iv]	In work mode
Irrational	Rational
Unscientific	Scientific
Collusive	Cooperative
Uncontrolled	Controlled
Unconscious	Conscious

"Do you think they are doing it, on purpose?" Jim asked

Kevin had to pause and think. "No, I don't think so. I think they are drawn into it. Unconscious. It's like giving a salesperson an office. You want them face-to-face with customers, but because they have an office, they have to go sit in it."

"So, what do you think the problem is?" Jim asked.

"I think, maybe, we need a communication seminar, see if we can get them on track," Kevin finally replied.

"I don't think you have a communication issue," Jim countered. "I think you have an accountability and authority issue."

Who is Accountable?

The Culture Club continued to meet. Sometimes thirty minutes, sometimes an hour each day. It was always a balance, define the work and execute the work.

"I have an issue where I could use your help," Jim explained to the group. "And I think your understanding will have impact all the way to the top of this organization.

"As a manager, you each have a team," he continued. "And you defined a manager as that person held accountable for the output of the team. So, if there is a decision to be made, related to the objective for that team, who is accountable for the consequences of that decision? Is it the manager, or the team?"

"Are you kidding me?" Johnny replied. "It's the manager. If it turns out to be a wrong decision, we don't fire the whole team, the manager is accountable."

"Then, whose decision is it to make?" Jim floated the question, the same question that frustrated Kevin DuPont. "Whose decision is it?"

"It's the manager's decision," Johnny responded. "The manager is accountable, the manager lives and dies by the decision."

"But what if the manager doesn't have all the facts to make an informed decision," Jim protested, "and needs the team to participate. Needs the team to gather the facts, analyze the facts. Then, whose decision is it?"

"It's still the manager's decision," Johnny persisted. "Look, if the team is seen as accountable, all hell breaks loose. People start covering their collective asses. Backpedaling. Blaming other people. If everyone is accountable, no one is accountable. It's still the manager's decision."

"But, what if the manager doesn't understand the technical facts to make a proper decision?" Jim was as persistent as Johnny.

"Jim, you know I am in charge of several technical service departments," Mary stepped in, "and you are also aware that I don't know one wrench from another. But I am still required to make decisions directly related to those technical operations, and I am held accountable for those decisions."

Jim nodded. "And?"

"And, I depend on my team to provide me with the best advice and full commitment to solving the problems we encounter every day in the department. I cannot afford to have people covering their ass, hedging their opinion or blaming other people. I need their undivided attention, technical counsel and direction. The only way I can be effective making those decisions is to listen and ask questions."

"That sounds nice in theory," Jim challenged. "But, you have to tell me how it works in real life."

"Okay. Here is one from last week," Mary explained. "We had an aircraft in for routine preventive maintenance. We spent a lot of time planning to make sure it would only be in the shop for one day. We finished the aircraft. It was three hours away from a scheduled departure, full load outbound. We got a service bulletin, critical.

"The maintenance supervisor read the bulletin and now had a dilemma. Should he put the plane back into the service hangar or does he release it to fly?

"He could pretend the aircraft was already released to the gate and that the service bulletin was too late. Flight operations would get the plane, the schedule would be met. Or the maintenance supervisor could pull the plane back in to the shop and create a small frenzy re-routing passengers. Whose decision?"

The group was quiet. Since this happened last week, everyone except Jim knew the answer.

"I'll bite, whose decision?"

Johnny jumped in to support. "The maintenance supervisor is accountable for getting the plane in and out of the shop. Flight operations is accountable to make sure passengers fly on schedule. We have a conflict. Someone has to make the decision. The maintenance supervisor wants to ground the plane, probably for another day. Flight operations wants to fly the plane. Whose decision is it?"

"You see, I don't know much about torque wrenches," Mary took over, "but my role, as manager, is to understand the context on both sides and make the decision. If it's the wrong decision, I am accountable. Understand, it's a short window to decide."

Jim continued to probe. "And?"

"And, I listened and asked questions," Mary answered. "The maintenance supervisor explained, critical means critical. I called the flight operations supervisor and explained critical. I asked for alternatives. There were three –

- Cancel the flight and re-route passengers.
- Delay the flight, scramble the crew for overtime to complete the repair, and get the aircraft to the gate late (hours late).
- Find a substitute aircraft.

"So, what happened?" Jim wanted to know.

"It doesn't matter what happened," Mary said. "What matters is that it was my decision and my decision alone. I was accountable for the decision and the consequences of the decision. The technical crew did their best to keep the aircraft in pristine working order. Flight operations did their best to keep the customers on schedule.

"If I decided to fly the plane and something happened, the technical crew would not be accountable. If I canceled the flight and the repair turned out to be a non-event, flight operations would not be accountable. This decision was my decision."

"What if the technical advice you get from your team is wrong?" Jim pressed.

"I am still accountable. As the manager, I have to evaluate the risk. If the risk is high, even if I trust my team to do their best, sometimes I have to double-check the data or bring in a second opinion on the analysis. I am still accountable."

"So, humor me," Jim chuckled. "What did you do?"

"Mary found another plane," Johnny piped in. "It was a different configuration, so the seating was a little screwed up and we had to kick off two dead-head flight attendants, but the passengers departed on time. We got the flight attendants on another airline, cost us a favor, but they made their turn as well."

Jim smiled and looked around the room at the Culture Club. "Thank you. I have my answer. By the way, I think we need to add a couple of more people to this group. I have a nomination from the white shirt crowd."

"You mean a VP?" Peter looked at Jim sideways.

Jim nodded. "Yes, a VP. Javier Ramirez. He's one of Al Ripley's crew, but he's not afraid to think out loud, his own thoughts. Check him out, ask around."

A Rose By Any Other Name

Kevin DuPont sat perched behind his desk, across from Jim Dunbar. "I think I have your answer," Jim began. "I want to make one small change to the *Executive Team Meeting*. We can try it out, see if it makes a difference. If it does, we can formally adopt it."

Kevin, for all of his youthful exuberance, was still disturbed by his exercise in democratic decision making. He was afraid he might become the designated symbol for command and control. He was afraid that he might become Al Ripley.

"This is a very subtle change," Jim assured him. "You have noble intentions for your executive team.

You want heavy participation in decision making. You want the buy-in that comes from participation, but you also find yourself accountable for those group decisions.

"In your role as President and CEO, you have an explicit agreement with the board of directors. You are accountable, the board contracted with you for a specific output. After Ripley's departure, your output is to stabilize the company, stem any short term bleeding and, if possible, turn a short term profit. The board doesn't need Outbound to hit a home run right now, but you are accountable to keep this company above break-even, in the black. No bold experiments, no risky plays. You are accountable."

"Yes," Kevin agreed. "But it seems I killed the morale of my executive team. When I told them they were accountable for the decisions made by the team, I thought it would create an esprit de corps, good for morale. I thought it would bring the team together. Instead, team members protected their turf. They formed small cliques that created friction and some poor decisions. Decisions that I am ultimately accountable for."

"That's the problem," Jim interrupted. "You can say the team is accountable, but, the team is not accountable, you are accountable. So, here is the change I want to make."

Kevin shifted in his chair, leaned forward.

"I want to change the name of the meeting," Jim announced. "From now on, the *Executive Team Meeting* will be called the *President's Meeting.*"ᵛ

The Agenda

"Only one item on the agenda, today," Kevin declared. "Jim Dunbar sits in our meetings, but he hasn't said much until today. Yesterday, Jim and I talked about the direction and purpose for this meeting, and he has some observations that I want him to explain."

"Thanks, Kevin," Jim took over. "In our last *Executive Team Meeting*, I noticed that some of you were upset by Kevin's decision to override some of your budget items. His explanation may have confused you.

"At the end of the day, when you all go home, Kevin is left with the accountability for the decisions made in this room. When Kevin arrived at Outbound Air, he suggested that this group would have the accountability for its own decisions, but he was wrong. As your manager, Kevin, alone, is accountable for your decisions.

"I spoke with Kevin. He feels the team has a morale issue. I told him the team doesn't have a morale issue, it has an accountability and authority issue. While the name of the meeting, the *Executive Team Meeting* describes the people in the room, it misrepresents who is accountable for the output of this team.

"I want to make one small change. From now on, the *Executive Team Meeting* will be known as the *President's Meeting*." Jim paused to let the thought settle in.

"Now, understanding that Kevin DuPont is accountable, to the board, for the output of this executive team, what changes?" Jim asked. "What changes about your role as you attend this meeting?"

There was a stunned silence.

Javier Ramirez cleared his throat. "I would say, it's about time. When Al Ripley was here, some of us didn't like him, but at least we knew who made the decisions. Ever since he left, we've drifted along, not losing ground, but not making headway either.

"I felt a little uncomfortable making some of the decisions in this meeting. I am pretty conservative, don't like a lot of risk, so sometimes, I hedge my bets. You may get an opinion out of me, but not necessarily the whole truth.

"If it's Kevin's decision, that changes everything for me. I can come clean with what I know, I can state the pros and the cons. I can come to this meeting without an axe to grind."

Javier sat down. Amazingly, no one else spoke. The air was thick. No one dared make eye contact. Jim had an awkward upside down feeling in his stomach.

Kevin couldn't stand the silence. "Well, that's it, good meeting. We're adjourned." He grabbed his blank pad of paper, his Mont Blanc pen and scurried for the door.

New to the Culture (Club)

Three days passed since the Culture Club met. A new face was at the table. Javier introduced himself. He knew Mary, but, not Peter, Frank and Johnny.

"I am Vice-President of Marketing," he began. "Our team works really hard driving traffic to our reservation portal. Every other airline had a head start, so, it has been a game of catch up. The only stroke of luck for us, is that the competition keeps acquiring each other and merging, so sometimes their eye is off the ball. Instead of making their reservation system better, they try to merge one system into the other. Creates customer confusion. And where there is confusion, there is opportunity, for us."

Frank stopped the small talk. "That's great, Javier, but what we want to know is how you got here to Outbound. Didn't you arrive with Al Ripley?"

Jim noticed the abrupt shift in the conversation. Jim recommended Javier join this group, so he wanted to jump in and defend. Johnny beat him to it.

"Hey, Frank. Let the guy catch his breath." Johnny turned to Javier and smiled. "Don't let Frank put you off with his directness. That's what we like about him. So, how did you get here to Outbound? Didn't you arrive with Al Ripley?"

That was it, the vase cracked in a moment of collective laughter. And it was Jim that joined the focused discussion. "Javier," he nodded. "I want to thank you for having the courage to join this group here. Lots of years with Outbound at this table. We are pretty upfront with each other, we don't hold back. So, tell us. What brought you here? Didn't you arrive with Al Ripley?"

At this point, even Javier smiled. He knew the group didn't want to hear about social media marketing or search engine optimization any more than he wanted to hear about technical service bulletins. "Yes, I got here with Al Ripley. Funny, I worked for him at another company, two full weeks before he transferred here. In the move, we heard that the entire executive team at Outbound quit the day the company sold. So, Al pulled some strings and brought his team with him. That included me. He said I looked good in a necktie."

Jim felt like someone drove an ice pick into his spinal cord. Sharp pain accompanied the inability to move. He wanted to scream that the executive team from Outbound was summarily sacked and that Al Ripley was the perpetrator. But the words got stuck somewhere between his lungs and his throat. Thank god he could still breathe.

Jim's body language was not lost on Javier. "Jim, are you okay. I know this was your company, but, you didn't know that your team tried to take the company down after the sale?"

Peter broke the tension of unspoken rage. "Javier, you have to realize something. I worked alongside those guys on the executive team for years. There is no way they would have tried to destroy Outbound. Ripley fired them before he even arrived."

It was Javier's turn to be confused. During his short tenure, he worked under the assumption that Outbound was a broken airline before Ripley took over. He looked carefully in the eyes of each person at the table. "So, why am I here? Why was I invited to join this group?"

All eyes looked at Jim. "I watched you on the executive team," he began. "You spoke up, the only one, and what you described was the truth in the room. You talked about things that everyone else on the team avoided. I knew it was so, because every time you opened your mouth, my stomach turned upside down. You have a knack for uncomfortable subjects. That's why this group needs you, even though they don't know you, yet."

"Okay," Javier replied after a moment. "That settles that. Then why are you all here? As I look around the room, there is an intensity that says you're not just here for the paycheck."

Presidential Debriefing

"So, what did you think?" Jim asked.

Kevin DuPont stared into the corner of the room, not making eye contact with Jim. "I am not sure. That was a pretty awkward meeting. Before it started, I agreed with you. I mean, all we did was change the name of the meeting. But I can put two and two together. I didn't like the reaction of the team."

"What did you expect?" Jim asked.

"I don't know. What did *you* expect?" Kevin replied.

"Exactly what we got. Panic. Except for Javier. He was the only calm head in the room. Of course, you cut the meeting short."

"Well, yes. Couldn't you feel the tension? Tough enough that morale is bad, now we have, what did you say, panic?"

Jim chuckled. "You young guys just don't have the patience. Didn't you know that all you had to do was outlast the panic?"

"Maybe," Kevin continued to stare. "I turned accountability over to the group, thinking they would come up with something. Now, it's back in my lap. I don't know where to start."

"Did you listen to Javier?"

Kevin broke out of his trance trying to recall. "He's the white shirt that stood up. No. I remember he talked, but I don't remember what he said."

"If you listen to your team, they will tell everything you need to know," Jim said quietly. "The team feels adrift, not losing ground, but not making headway. They are looking for direction. They are looking for direction from you."

"But, I am just the interim CEO. I'm not here forever. I am only a place marker. I am supposed to sit in the chair while the board finds someone to come in and take over permanently."

Jim's head dropped back with this new piece of data. "What do you mean, you are just a placeholder? I understand what a placeholder is, what does that mean for the company?"

"You didn't know?" Though he never told anyone, even Kevin was surprised that Jim, the Chief Culture Officer didn't know. "The board uses me exclusively on assignments for six months or less. I have very direct orders to not rock the boat. I am a buffer that gives the board time. Kind of like Ripley. He almost always goes in after a merger. His purpose is to reduce costs, drive as much profitability as possible. His bonus is based on the incremental difference in the bottom line post acquisition. But, this is the second time I followed after him, to tread water while the board tries to figure out his mess.

"As far as strategic direction, I have no clue." Kevin went still, breathing deep. "I have no strategy beyond the next couple of months."

Missing

Jim sat alone in the coffee room, waiting for the others. Mary and Javier entered at the same time. "Good morning," Jim perked up.

"Good morning," Mary replied, noticing Jim's demeanor. "Why the long face?"

Jim surveyed the walls of the room. Many of the drawings they made, were photographed, laminated and now on display. "We've talked, for the past few months, about how a group works together. And, I don't mean gets together for a pint at the pub, but gets together to get work done. It's all well, and good, but there is something missing."

He had Javier's attention, as Frank and Johnny sat down. Peter finished a phone call just outside the door. "We talked about roles, how to measure the complexity of a role by looking at its longest time span task. We talked about the capability required to be effective in that role. We talked about the way roles connect to each other in managerial relationships. We talked about accountability and authority, and that accountability rests with the manager. This is all good stuff, but something is missing, and I didn't realize it until yesterday."

"What's that?" Mary asked.

"Javier asked the question the first time he sat in with the group. Why are we here? And I don't mean, why are you here, Mary, why is Mary here? I mean, why is Outbound here? What do we do?"

"Well, we run an airline, that's what we do," Johnny replied.

"Lots of companies run airlines," Jim pressed. "Why do *we* run an airline?"

"To be the best airline," Peter chimed in, sliding his cellphone into his pocket. "We do things differently, that's why our customers like us. They like, how we do, what we do."

"That's *how* we run an airline," Jim continued. "The question is *why* do we run an airline? And that's what is missing."

There was no convenient chart or graph on the white board. This was not something to be numbered I, II, III, IV. "I didn't realize it was missing until yesterday," Jim nodded, looking carefully around the room. "I assumed it was there. I thought it was hung on the wall with all the teamwork posters. But it wasn't. It's gone missing." Jim's eyes rested on Javier. "You said it."

Javier conspicuously tried to figure out what Jim was thinking.

"With the executive group, in the President's Meeting," Jim continued. "You said you felt adrift."

Javier finally nodded. "Yes, not losing ground, not making headway. Without direction."

Jim stayed quiet. He could have filled the void. The air got thick. His stomach began to turn. Was Javier the only one who noticed? Wait. He watched as the shift began, the onset of panic. Outlast the panic. Jim noticeably breathed deep, and he saw Frank breathe deep, Mary followed suit. The tension vanished and the group leaned in. Not a word. This group was comfortable with the tension. It did not scare them.

"Kevin," Javier slowly called out the name. "It's Kevin's job to define the direction."

That's when Jim broke the silence. "It's not coming from Kevin. Kevin is toast."

Part Seven

Secret Communique

Fran Smith was like an early warning signal. She was the lead dog on all mergers and acquisitions. Though not a member of the board, she seemed to know exactly what they thought, and she knew with whom to share it.

Fran communicated mostly by phone. Emails were too easily copied and forwarded. Sensitive information was better left without a trace. Her conversation with Jim Dunbar was short and sweet.

"The hunt is on," Fran explained. "And there are two people on the short list to replace Kevin DuPont. One is Catherine Nibali."

Catherine Nibali was rare in the corporate world. She shattered more than one glass ceiling. Unassuming in a negotiation, disarming with her lure, in between the lines of a contract, she almost always got her way. Catherine Nibali was the outside candidate. Coriolis was aloof in their approach, the requisite background search, a private investigator.

Catherine was four years into her third company as a hired CEO. Each enterprise she touched, accelerated its growth, and even after her departure, continued to outperform competitors. On each exit, there was a competent replacement in the wings, an insider who stepped into a seamless transition. The culture under her watch and the culture after she left, remarkably the same. She left a permanent mark on each company she inhabited.

The interview process was discreet and highly confidential. The instability created by a shakeup at the top was not welcome by Coriolis or the candidates on the short list, until, of course, there was certainty in the selection of a successor.

"Coriolis also has an inside candidate," Fran continued. "Al Ripley." She anticipated Jim's response, but he was quiet.

Because he was still under contract, Al Ripley was farmed out like an old racehorse waiting for the glue factory. To keep him busy, and out of trouble, his assignment landed him with a lazy manufacturing company producing chemical compounds. Forty seven years of history saw this once vibrant enterprise consumed by government regulation over ozone depletion and fluorocarbons. The company survived, but only as a former shadow of itself. An environmental discovery in an abandoned septic tank on the property was the last straw. Coriolis attempted to sell the entity out of its portfolio, but no one wanted the liability for the cleanup. It seemed a suitable place to ship Al Ripley. Put him on the farm to live out his days where he could do no further damage.

And that was the wrinkle in Al Ripley's character. Put him in a dirt hole and he would discover gold. In the few short months since his retreat from Outbound Air, in this languishing chemical factory, Ripley discovered two patents and a proprietary formula tied to a government contract. If anyone knew how to play a government contract, it was Al Ripley. He gutted the company, laid off all the employees, sold the patents, tripling Coriolis' original investment. The property was mothballed through a local brownfield initiative, high fences and forbidding signs. Case closed, Al spent most afternoons playing golf.

Even the stigma of the Outbound crash had settled. An anonymous source inside the NTSB leaked that, though its probe would not be resolved for months, so far, its findings were inconclusive to anything other than pilot error. While Ripley was no darling in the mind of the board, he lobbied heavily to get back in the game at Outbound Air.

Jim Dunbar was predictably troubled by the news. The earn-out period in his sale of Outbound to Coriolis was half expired and there was no progress in passenger revenue miles toward the earn-out he was to receive. He now understood why earn-out money was the curse inside most acquisition agreements. Jim Dunbar was on the journey to a 50/50 possibility of his former company back under the thumb of Al Ripley.

Direction

"Toast?" Johnny asked. "You mean he got fired?"

"Not fired," Jim explained. "Kevin made the announcement today in an email to his executive team. He was reassigned. Each member of the executive team is free to make their own announcement down the line."

Javier looked puzzled. "I am a member of the executive team. I didn't get the email."

"That's because you scare the crap out of him," Jim chuckled.

"When?" Peter wanted to know.

"Four weeks. The board is finishing their search for a successor." Jim made no more explanation. He would not publicly entertain the possibility of Ripley's return.

"One more thing," Jim concluded. "At some point, we expect a new CEO. In the meantime, let's not wait. Let's not think that the new CEO will arrive and everything will be saved. We talked about direction. Let's focus on that. Why do we run an airline? What's so special about *what* we do, *how* we do it and *why* we do it?"

At the Helm

"Welcome," Catherine proclaimed. "So, you are my executive team and, as I understand it, this is the *President's Meeting*. Not sure whose notion that was, but I like it.

"You run a decent airline operation here. I did some research, and this company has the potential to be a *great* airline. First thing you need to know about me, is that I don't know anything about running an airline. My background is in hospitality. We put our customers to sleep at night, but when they wake up, they are still in the same place. When your customers nod out, they wake up in an entirely different place. But, I assume you will teach me all I need to know.

"It's an honor to have the founder of this company, Jim Dunbar, in the room. He has the role of Chief Culture Officer. I don't know what that means, either, but I am sure someone thought it was a good idea.

"We have a lot of work to do, and a sense of urgency. Decent airlines go out of business all the time. And, often, when they go out of business, no one can explain *why*. And that's the point. No one can explain *why*. No one can explain *why* that airline was in business in the first place.

"Lots of people can run an airline. A decent airline can tell you *how* they run it, but only a great airline can tell you *why*. I don't know *why*, and that is the first thing we have to figure out together.

"Between now and tomorrow morning at 10:00am, your assignment is sit down and think about *why* we are in business. I suggest you write it down, because in the heat of the moment tomorrow at 10:00am, you will forget your ideas.

"Over the next eight days, I plan to spend two hours with each of you. In that time, you will explain to me your role in this company and why it is necessary and how it fits in with the rest of the organization.

"If there are no other questions, this *President's Meeting* is adjourned."

Jim Dunbar sat in silence. He endured the tenure of Al Ripley. He sat through the blip of Kevin DuPont. Catherine Nibali was going to be interesting.

The Why Meeting

Sitting around the table, with cherub faces, sat the executive team. In front, neatly stapled, they each had a few sheets of paper with varying lengths of narrative.

"Make no mistake about this," Catherine began the meeting. "With all due respect to friendly skies, the skies are NOT friendly. All this pampering and pillow fluffing, is just a ruse. Jim Dunbar explained it to me. Here is what we do. We cram 70 or so people into a giant metal tube. We hurl that tube at 400 miles an hour through the sky and somehow, through the grace of relatively tiny wheels and some giant shock absorbers, we manage to put the tube back on the ground without killing anybody. Except once. That's what we do.

"How we do it is magic," she continued. "I can figure out how a boat floats, or how a car rolls down the highway, but I have no idea how we keep a few tons of heavy metal in the air for hours. Definitely magic," she paused.

"But *what* we do and *how* we do it are not the questions for today. I want to know *why*? Because if we don't know why, we will never be a great airline. What is our mission?"

Catherine was standing for this soliloquy, but took the pause to walk around the room and take an empty seat halfway down the side, leaving the head of the table open.

Javier would normally leap into the fray at this moment, but he had been watching Jim Dunbar for some weeks now, and decided not to go first.

The silence in the room grew.

"Can I borrow a pen, anyone have a pen?" Catherine whispered. "I might want to take some notes."

Still no takers for the forward position at the head of the table.

"Paper, anyone have a sheet of paper?" Catherine filled the space, looking around, preparing to listen. "Come on, now. I can see every one of you has a neatly typewritten paper ready for today. We just need someone to go first."

No one made eye contact. No one spoke. Javier was tempted.

"Right then. I'll go first," Catherine spoke. "I believe that the reason we are in business is to be the research and development wing of the company that will mount the first manned space venture to the planet Mars. And what we do here, is practice for that mission."

At first, there was total denial that the words they heard were the words that were said. Then, there was acknowledgment, with snickers, that the words were, indeed, said, but a denial that it was the new CEO who said them. A quarter of a minute passed, then all hell broke loose in the room. The stifled amusement turned to chorus laughter punctuated by an anonymous snort.

"What do you think, Jim?" Catherine asked.

Jim stood up quietly as everyone regained composure. "That's exactly what I had in mind when I started this airline."

As he sat down, the head shaking began. Sideways glances. A snort that was finally identified. For a provincial group of white buttoned down shirts, they sure knew how to have a good time.

"Seriously, someone get up there on the white board and write this stuff down," Catherine instructed. A sheepish volunteer stepped up. "Go on. M-A-R-S, Mars. Write it down. Who has the next idea?"

The next idea was a serious attempt about transporting people to faraway places, too far to drive.

"That's not funny," Catherine announced. "If you think you have a good idea, it has to be funny."

The room lightened up. Ideas began to flow. Forty five minutes later, eighty-two ideas filled the board. The scribe was the center of attention. Catherine stood up.

"Now, some of these ideas are really stupid," she observed. "That one about Mars, stupid. Cross it off. Who has a smart phone?"

Everyone had a smart phone.

"Take a picture. Take a picture of the board," she prompted. "Everybody, take a picture of the board. Now, go home tonight and study the board. Somewhere in there are some good ideas. Right? Tomorrow, same time, back in here. I want to know what you think. *President's Meeting* adjourned."

The First Cut

"I heard this was your idea," Catherine walked into Jim's office, closing the door. "The *President's Meeting*. Your idea?"

"You are correct. It was my idea. It had its purpose with Kevin DuPont," Jim replied.

"I told you, I like it," Catherine responded. "It lets everyone know why they are in the meeting, to help me."

"Sounds a little self-centered," Jim observed.

"Not at all, helping someone can be very fulfilling," Catherine replied. "And, I am going to need a lot of help. I have some very important decisions to make in the next few days. I started my round of interviews. Three quarters of the executive team will be reassigned. They don't belong."

"How can you tell? You have only been here for three days," Jim questioned.

"Come on, Jim, you know these folks. Take Javier Ramirez, he's a keeper. You spotted him, just like I did. He told me about this group you created called the Culture Club, how you meet together to define roles and levels of work. Bright guy. And I bet there are more like him in this company, but they are hidden away. And most of the executive team, I don't know where they came from or who picked them, but we have to move them out."

"We?" Jim looked at Catherine.

"Yes, we. You started this company. I didn't have to scratch very far to get the skinny on what this company was like before Coriolis bought it. You think you are here because of an earn-out in your contract. But, if you are honest with yourself, you are here, because this is your baby and someone else tried to kill it. So, yes. *We. We* have some work to do."

Mission Critical

The WHY Meeting reconvened. Some completed their homework. Others coasted. Javier Ramirez was prepared. The group settled on two concepts, but they were stuck. The group could not figure out if the airline was for the business traveler or the vacation traveler, two very distinct groups with different travel needs.

"I have to decide," Catherine pressed. "So, give me your best thinking. Do we run an airline for business travelers that occasionally gets boarded by vacationers? Or do we run a vacation airline that occasionally gets boarded by business travelers?"

"Why can't we do both?" Javier asked. "Look, things have changed. The business traveler used to board an airplane in a suit with a briefcase. They carried file folders with papers and spreadsheets to read in the plane. As soon as they landed, they sped away to a meeting. They wanted to sit in first class so they could get on the plane first and not have to stand in line with a bunch of whiny kids and grandpa who take twenty minutes to get down the jetway.

"Well, the business papers are gone, because now they carry laptops and tablets. The laptops are small enough and have enough battery, so they can work coast to coast on any reasonable tray table. Company travel departments won't pay for first class, but our passengers still don't want their knees buried in the back of the seat in front. Even business dress is more casual. You can still tell the business traveler from the vacationer, but the silk tie is a lot less frequent.

"And, then we have the vacationer. Families travel together, friends travel together, but look at them. They're all buried in their smart phones. They would rather text each other across the plane than talk. If you pay no attention to the way the passengers are dressed, you can't tell them apart."

There was a new face sitting in the room. Mary spent most of her career at Outbound as the technical services manager, but in the past 24 hours, she was invited to join the executive team. "If we create too much of a vacation atmosphere, don't you think the business traveler will be put off? The reason the vacationer is on the plane and the reason the business traveler is on the plane are different."

"Are they?" Javier countered. "Mary, the last time you took vacation, did you carry your smartphone with you?"

Mary nodded, "Yes."

"And I am wondering," Javier continued. "Did you also take your laptop?"

Mary continued to nod.

"And, on vacation, did you wake up every morning and check your email?"

Mary's nod now contained a smile, "Yes."

"So, you were on vacation, but you were still tied to your smartphone and laptop?" He did not stop for her to answer. "It would be interesting for marketing to play around with the combination of the idea of a vacation airline for the business traveler."

Catherine listened, but interrupted. "Great discussion, but we have to focus on a single mission. We cannot be all things to all people. If our focus is the business traveler, that doesn't mean we won't have some vacationers on board, but, our mission will help us define what drives our revenue." She looked around the room. "This strategy will help us structure the rest of the company, but we have to define the mission first. Who has the next idea?"

As the meeting continued, Jim watched Catherine. Not only did she push the meeting along, but she carefully gauged participation and contribution. It was very clear to Jim, she was rebuilding her executive team.

Horsepower

It was just the two of them with two lists of names, a short list and a long list. "I want to identify the high potentials," Catherine told Jim. "We're going to need a lot of horsepower to move this company forward."

"Yes, I have been looking at the org chart that Al Ripley used. Kevin DuPont left it largely unchanged," Jim observed.

"You can toss that org chart," Catherine replied. "Who knows the logic behind it? Too early to draw up an org chart anyway. First, we have to settle on a mission, then choose our core function and supporting functions. And some of those functions are more complex than others. I believe your Culture Club calls it level of work. Once we identify those functions and figure out the level of work in each function, then we can define the roles for an org chart. These steps have an order to them."

Organizational Steps
- Strategy – define vision, mission, business model.
- Identify the main operational functions.
- Identify the support functions.
- In each function, identify the level of work required.
- For each level of work, identify the necessary roles by title.
- In each role, identify the effectiveness of the person in the role.

"I see," Jim said, agreeing with Catherine, though he didn't see it as clearly as Catherine did. It was interesting, he thought, she had a very structured approach to her first few days at Outbound, but she also integrated ideas from the Culture Club.

"Oh, and one more thing," she continued. "I need you to kill the Culture Club."

Jim was stunned. Over the past few months, in the pressure cooker of turmoil, the Culture Club was one place he found comfort. It was a place where the group could explore ideas and learn. The Culture Club produced a clearer understanding of decision making and problem solving. It bonded a group of managers together against the insanity of Al Ripley and the ineptness of Kevin DuPont. Catherine's arrival was a breath of fresh air, but now she wanted to kill the very thing that allowed Jim to survive.

"Are you sure?" his protest began. "The Culture Club has been doing some very important work. It's the one bright spot in this company, for me."

"It's an outlier," Catherine quickly replied. "And it was totally necessary under Al Ripley. It could not have existed any other way except as an outlier group. That's why, now, it has to stop."

"But, they are working on some things that, I think, will be helpful in the process you just described. Deciding core functions, support functions, level of work. I mean, the idea of level of work never occurred to me before the group started to meet."

"Oh, the group is going to continue to meet," Catherine assured him. "But, not as an outlier. The focus of the group is exactly what we need right now. They have to understand this thinking is not something to be done in the coffee room before and after hours. This is the work that has to be done to re-design this company, from the inside. This is precisely the managerial work I need them doing. This is on-the-clock thinking, not outlier thinking. The ad-hoc charts you have down in the coffee room. I want those charts brought into the conference room."

Jim didn't quite know what to say.

"And, for now, I want to add Peter, Frank and Johnny to the short list. I want them in the executive team meetings. And this other list. These people are going in for cross training. They are off the executive team. We need to find some other place in the company for them to be productive. Or we need them out."

Mission Stated

"First, I want to thank you all, for your input over the past few meetings. It was important to identify the strategy to pursue. Based on your feedback, and ideas and arguments, our focus will be on the serious business traveler. Historically, that is how Jim Dunbar started this airline. It's also a big enough market. Our commuter jets are smaller than the jumbos, they are fuel efficient. We can adjust our load factors and routes faster than some of the bigger airlines."

Catherine looked around the room, paying particular attention to Javier Ramirez. She knew the stories about Kevin DuPont and his democratic decision making and knew that Javier was the only team member to stand up when Kevin betrayed his promise.

Javier's idea of placating both the business traveler and the vacation traveler was nowhere in this rendition of the mission statement. "Javier?" Catherine raised her eyebrows looking for a response.

Javier was smiling. During the discussions, he was the heaviest participant. One meeting, he argued against himself just to look at the ideas in a different way. "I am satisfied," he responded. "I appreciate the process. It was hard work. Knowing that this was your decision, allowed me to dig in without trying to protect my own agenda. In one sense, this process was exhausting, but I am ready to charge ahead."

"So, that's our strategy," Catherine pressed. "I will let the marketing department wordsmith it, but for now, let's just say our focus will be on the business traveler."

There was a general rustle in the conference room. It was evident that stomachs began to relax, the air was comfortable, and the room was safe. That lasted about ten seconds.

"Next assignment," Catherine launched, "is to determine our main function. If our mission is to focus on the business traveler, what is our core function? And you know me by now. No fluff. As we define this, it has to specific and understandable.

"I know you have some day-to-day stuff to attend to, so this meeting is adjourned. Reconvene tomorrow with your thoughts. Oh, one more thing. I expect you to get together and trade your ideas with each other, ad hoc. This is a collaborative effort. See you tomorrow."

It was a short meeting, but no one grumbled as they left the room.

Core Function

"Before we get started today, I want to remind you of the purpose of this meeting. We, as a group, need to clearly define the core function of this airline, then define all the support functions. Jim Dunbar has cleverly named this meeting, *the President's Meeting*, so I want to make it clear. I am accountable to the Board of Directors, so at the end of the day, I am accountable for this decision. This decision will establish the structure of the company. This structure will govern the way we work together."

Contributions for core function were written on large white-boards. Jim Dunbar killed the Culture Club in the space of ten minutes, dismantled the white boards in the coffee room and hung them in the conference room. He did not tell the Culture Club of its demise, but readily apparent, its purpose shifted from outlier to mainstream, optically hard wired to the frontal lobe of the CEO.

Ideas flew onto the board. Catherine suspended all rational thought, so every idea was recorded without judgment. Ideas exhausted, they were grouped into six different categories. Volunteers took up the cause of each category and worked to distill the ideas into six separate functions, each of which was a candidate for the airline's *core* function. Each function had a small group ready to defend.

"Perfect," Catherine proclaimed. "Each group here has identified its candidate for core function. Now, look to your right and shift. Each group will take the idea from the group to its right. You will have thirty minutes to debrief each other, handing the idea off so the new team can advocate."

There was first, disbelief, that each team would have to advocate for another position, but within 60 seconds, the room grew loud with unformatted discussion.

Catherine motioned Jim into the hallway. "Interesting approach," Jim observed as they watched through the window in the conference room door.

"You will notice that I gave them conflicting directions," Catherine mused. "They have to learn about the next group's idea while they are explaining their own idea to yet, another group. I want them to understand that no idea will emerge the winner without the collaboration and understanding of other people on the executive team."

Thirty minutes went quickly. Each team had five minutes to make their case for the airline's core function. In the end, it was Javier who made the most compelling argument. "At first, I lined up behind the business traveler's cabin experience," he started, "but, then, you made my group advocate for safe travel on schedule. I changed my mind. The business traveler doesn't fly with us because of our cabin experience, though that will certainly be a supporting function. The business traveler has something important to do on the ground at the destination. That purpose is likely an appointment, a scheduled meeting, a sales call. The most important thing is that we get the business traveler safely to the destination on schedule. During our discussion, someone told the story about packing passengers into a metal tube, hurling that tube through the air at 400 miles per hour and, at the appointed time, safely putting it back on the ground. If we screw that up, nothing else matters. To make that happen will require high coordination of our internal systems and subsystems in the face of outside factors like weather and air traffic."

Each group made their best case. It was now up to Catherine Nibali to make the decision. "Right then, our mission is to support the business traveler. Our core function is safe travel on schedule."

Each member of the new executive management team exchanged approving glances. They did not all agree, but they participated in the process. In the end, people support a decision they help to make.

"Back in your groups," Catherine instructed. "While we worked to identify our core function, we talked about a number of other things we do, that *support* our core function. Most of them, we have already hashed out, they're on the boards around the room. Some of you currently work directly inside those functions. For the next two hours, I want you to work together to attach our support functions to the core function. Javier, the room is yours."

Catherine grabbed Jim's attention and motioned him out the door. "Let them work this part out," she said. "Plenty of capability in the room for these decisions."

"So, the big decision was made. You're calling it a day?" Jim asked.

"Pretty much. Set the direction, get the right team in place. Mind you, they will run up against more difficulty in this process, so you and I will be back in the room, but, for now, we can get some coffee."

"One question," Jim was curious. "How do you know that the core function of the airline should be safe travel on schedule?"

Catherine smiled. "You told me first, then the team came to the same conclusion."

"But, I didn't say anything in the room."

"Jim, when you started the airline, think back, in the beginning, it was just a hobby. It was your passion." She paused long enough for Jim to nod.

"But, at some point," Catherine continued, "your airline turned into a business. One day you flew friends back and forth, the next day, you became an airline. What happened to make that change?"

Even though the time frame was almost three decades in the past, Jim could remember it like yesterday. He had to chuckle. "When I flew my friends, it was like a charter, never an empty airplane. We flew when the passengers wanted to go. Then one day, I sent out an email that I intended to fly on a schedule, so my passengers could make their travel plans."

"What happened?" Catherine prompted.

"That was the first trip that my plane flew empty. I had a scheduled return, so, I had to dead-head to the next airport."

"And, that's the moment Outbound became an airline," Catherine smiled. That's how I knew that our core function was safe travel on schedule."

Level of work

With the mission defined, the core function and the support functions defined, Catherine convened the next meeting. "I know you are all accountable for making sure this airline continues to operate while we sit in this room, working through this function stuff. So, I have a question for you. How do your teams know what to do today?"

Nervous glances went around the table, not even Javier could figure out where this was going. "Come on, you arrived at work this morning and came straight away into this meeting. Your teams are all out there, without you, making decisions and solving problems. How do they know what to do today?"

Finally, Peter spoke up. "Sounds too obvious, but my team is mostly doing their work today, the same as they did, yesterday."

"And, if I hold you in this room, through tomorrow, how will they know what to do tomorrow?"

Peter was on a roll. "I suppose they will carry on tomorrow the same way they carried on today, the same way they carried on yesterday." He looked around to see if anyone else appreciated his humor.

"Right then, if your teams can carry on the same way tomorrow, then what do I need you for?" Catherine stared sternly in the eyes of her executive team.

Peter looked around to see if someone else might fill the void of silence. It was Mary's turn. "You are absolutely right. My team can carry on the same way, day after day. And they can make decisions and they can solve problems, as long as those decisions and problems are the same as yesterday. But, here's the rub. Something is going to change. It might be a weather system, a mechanical delay, or a broken flight connection. Something is going to change and that's when they will need me."

"Exactly," Catherine beamed. "As long as nothing changes, your teams do not need you. They can handle all the routine decisions and problems. But, you know that something *will* change, something always changes. This airline operates in a world of uncertainty. You helped define a number of standard operating procedures. Your teams know how to handle weather systems, flight delays and lost baggage. They know how to re-route customers. They even know what to do in the event of a computer outage or a security breach."

Catherine stopped to let this sink in, before she continued.

"But, what happens when our load factors on a route fall below the level of profitability for a thirty day period. Should they cancel all the flights?"

A wave covered the room. Some stared down at the table, some stared at the ceiling. They did not avoid eye contact, but, instead, looked inside to connect to some logical response. Javier broke the silence. "No," he was emphatic. "First, that is a decision they do *not* have the authority to make."

"And, why not. The routes are unprofitable, why shouldn't your shift supervisors cancel those flights?" Catherine challenged.

"It's not their role to make a decision like that?" Javier replied.

"Says who?" Catherine baited.

An awkward twenty seconds ticked by on the clock. "Says me," Javier finally relented. "That is not a decision that my shift supervisors are capable of making."

"And, who appointed you to make that decision?" Catherine continued to press.

"You did," Javier replied without hesitation. "My shift supervisors are perfectly capable of handling the day to day uncertainty of running an airline, but the problem of an unprofitable route likely has nothing to do with operations. It could be a marketing problem, a pricing problem. It could be a new competitor. It could be a spike in fuel costs. It could be the discovery of a new oil field in North Dakota, or government throttling of fracking activity. All of those issues could impact passenger load factors and are beyond the level of work of my shift supervisors.

"Look," Javier continued, "if our core function is *safe* air travel on *schedule*, we have to look long and hard before we go canceling flights. Our route planning looks out two years, at a minimum. We analyze all kinds of data as we plan gate to gate. Load factors, demographics, business trends, fuel and competition. It all goes into the mix."

"Now, we are getting somewhere," Catherine mused. "Would you all agree that when we look at our core function and the support functions, inside each function are different levels of work? And we can see those levels of work in the decisions that are made and the problems that are solved."

The fog in the room began to clear.

Decisions and Problems

"First, let's look at the charts we brought up from the coffee room," Catherine continued. "This group worked for several months, precisely on our next step. Level of work has been accurately identified by looking at the time span of the goals and objectives in the role. But are there other characteristics we need to look at?"

"Absolutely," Peter chimed in. "Take a look at this chart here. If you start at the bottom, you can see some things line up that are helpful. See what you think?"

Properties in Levels of Work[vi]						
Level of Work	Longest Time Span Goals	Typical Managerial Role	Function	Tools	Problem Solving	Value
S – I	1d-3m	Production Technician Labor Clerical	Production	Real tools, equipment.	Trial and Error	Quality

"It doesn't matter what department," Frank added. "The level of work is that same whether it's clerical, baggage handling or customer service work. They have different skills but the time span of their tasks is in the same range."

"Wait, you are telling me that a baggage handler is the same level of work as customer service?" Catherine challenged.

"Within the range," Johnny replied. "We talked all night about this one. At first blush, you might think that a baggage handler isn't very high up on the food chain. But think about the discretionary judgment that team has to use. They have problems to solve and decisions to make as they maneuver portable conveyors in and around multi-million dollar aircraft. What happens if they misjudge and push a machine one inch into the skin of an airplane? Or if they fail to fasten a baggage door? Or if they are careless about the way cargo and equipment is secured inside the belly? Remember ValuJet?"

The somber reference to the 1996 airline disaster that killed 110 aboard fell over the group.

Catherine broke the silence. "I get it, now. You're right. We are in the life and death business."

"Even still," Peter continued, "the solutions to these problems can be trained. In most cases, while people's lives depend on them, the decisions are repetitive. The work is tangible and concrete. The cargo door is closed or it's open. There is little ambiguity. While planes may be early or late, and switch gates without notice, the time span of the problems to be solved is short."

"So, talk to me about customer service," Catherine asked. "It still seems like a higher level of work."

"Yes, high level I. Remember, it's the longest task in the role that calibrates the level of work in the role. Customer service has to understand our computer systems and be trained on what steps to take to solve a customer problem. While our customers think their delayed flight or missed connection is unique, solving that problem has a limited number of solutions. While flight times change, the uncertainty is short term."

"Look at level II," Johnny prompted. "Sometimes, it's easier to understand one level of work by looking at other levels of work."

Properties in Levels of Work						
Level of Work	Longest Time Span Goals	Typical Managerial Role	Function	Tools	Problem Solving	Value
S – II	3-12m	Supervisor Project Manager Coordinator Project Engineer	Makes sure production gets done, implements the production system	Schedules, checklists, meetings.	Experience, manuals, best practices	Accurate, complete, on-time.
S – I	1d-3m	Production Technician Labor Clerical	Production	Real tools, equipment.	Trial and Error	Quality

"Talk to me about Level II," Catherine asked.

"The time span of the goals increase," Johnny pointed out. "And a shift in the tools. Most of our supervisor roles function to make sure our production work gets done, whether it's on-board catering or take-offs and landings. They use schedules, checklists and meetings to make sure the production work is done accurately, completely and on-time. Given a problem to solve, they are adept at applying our standard procedures and best-practice manuals."

"And, so, what happens if load factors on a route fall below the level of profitability for a thirty day period?" Catherine repeated. "Why shouldn't the shift supervisor cancel the flights? A thirty day window is certainly within the time span on the chart."

"It's a thirty day window, but it's not a thirty day problem and certainly not a thirty day decision," Javier replied. "Routes take months and years to build. A decision to cancel a route is a big decision."

"How big of a decision?" Catherine challenged.

"Look at the time span impact of the decision," Javier smiled, realizing that Catherine was teaching the group about a concept the Culture Club struggled to define. "There are big decisions and small decisions we all make. We can actually measure the size of the decision by looking at its impact over time."

"So, you are telling the group," Catherine prompted, "that if we can measure the impact of a decision over time, we can determine in which level of work the decision should be made."

"Exactly," Javier nodded.

"Let's look at Level III," Catherine said.

Properties in Levels of Work						
Level of Work	Longest Time Span Goals	Typical Managerial Role	Function	Tools	Problem Solving	Value
S – III	1-2y	Manager	Creates system. Monitors system. Improves system.	Flowcharts, sequence, planning.	Root cause analysis, comparative analysis	Single system efficiency, consistency, predictability
S – II	3-12m	Supervisor Project Manager Coordinator Project Engineer	Makes sure production gets done, implements the production system	Schedules, checklists, meetings.	Experience, manuals, best practices	Accurate, complete, on-time.
S – I	1d-3m	Production Technician Labor Clerical	Production	Real tools, equipment.	Trial and Error	Quality

"The time span of the goals and objectives gets longer," Mary explained. "One to two years into the future. The problems and decisions at this level of work are surrounded by uncertainty. To cancel a route because load factors are low is a big decision. It's not black or white. The risk is high. There is uncertainty. The reasons for a change in load factors can come from a number of sources, lots of variables. The shift supervisor at Level II, faced with a problem, may be expert at applying our standard operating procedures. But there is no best practice when load factors fall. We don't have a procedure for that."

"Why don't we have a procedure for that?" Catherine prodded.

"Because the reason for the change in load factor may be different every time. The uncertainty surrounding this decision is not something that can be looked up in our process documentation. We have to collect new data, analyze that data and then use our best judgment."

"And, how will we know we made the best decision?" Catherine asked.

"That's just it," Mary replied. "It's a judgment. If the decision was a calculation that a computer could make, between known factors, then we would let the computer make the calculation. A decision is a judgment made in the face of ambiguity and uncertainty. The further into the future, the more uncertainty."

"And, you are suggesting we can measure that uncertainty by simply looking at the time span of the goal?" Catherine wanted to confirm.

"It has everything to do with the target completion time," Peter jumped back in the conversation. "If we have a project that is due tomorrow afternoon, what is the likelihood that we know exactly which team members will work on that project? We can call them by name. What is the likelihood that we know exactly what materials will be used on that project? What is the likelihood that we are already in possession of those materials? What is the likelihood that we already have those materials staged and ready to go? What is the likelihood we know precisely what time, within fifteen minutes that the project will be delivered?"

As Peter looked around, he could see the heads nodding in agreement. "So, why do we know all that stuff? Why are all of the elements of that project so concrete and tangible?" Peter stopped. "There is one very simple reason we have to know all that stuff. The project is due tomorrow afternoon.

"But, if we have a project," he continued, "that is 18 months out, what is the possibility that someone on our team, during the next 18 months, might quit, retire or move to Montana? What is the possibility that our equipment supplier might go bankrupt, or have some interruption in their supply chain in the next 18 months? What is the possibility that we might get a call from a government agency inspecting our process, telling us that we have to use an alternate process? What is the possibility that somewhere along the line, during the next 18 months, there will be some change in the project specification? The longer the project, the more there is uncertainty.

"And if I am the project manager, you expect me to have contingency plans for all those potential problems. Murphy's Law says, anything that *can* go wrong, *will* go wrong. Murphy is alive and well, but Murphy is no excuse. You expect me to deal with it. Because one thing did not change, the completion date." Peter took a breath.

Catherine was pleased with the understanding of her team. "It appears that something else changed about the *function* of this role. Tell me about this level III system focus."

Properties in Levels of Work						
Level of Work	Longest Time Span Goals	Typical Managerial Role	Function	Tools	Problem Solving	Value
S – III	1-2y	Manager	Creates system. Monitors system. Improves system.	Flowcharts, sequence, planning.	Root cause analysis, comparative analysis	Single system efficiency, consistency, predictability .
S – II	3-12m	Supervisor Project Manager Coordinator Project Engineer	Makes sure production gets done, implements the production system	Schedules, checklists, meetings.	Experience, manuals, best practices	Accurate, complete, on-time.
S – I	1d-3m	Production Technician Labor Clerical	Production	Real tools, equipment.	Trial and Error	Quality

Mary, Peter, Frank, Johnny and Javier looked at each other, appearing to draw straws. Frank got the nod. "The level III manager is not only concerned about the production work getting done, but also the *way* it is being done. This is more than defining our methods and processes. This manager is looking at consistency and predictability, so that every time we do something, the output is the same."

"Take on-time departures," Mary said. "It's our core function. We want predictability prior to departure to make sure the plane leaves on time. Sure, we could all run around like chickens and for the most part, the plane would leave on time. But, with a system, we can work calmly, and consistently make the push-off at the gate on schedule. We need the system to prevent problems, to make sure the most efficient sequence is followed every time."

"Give me an example," Catherine said.

"We always load wheelchair passengers, first," Mary replied. "We have to maneuver the chairs down the jetway and get passengers from the wheelchair to their seat. If other passengers load at the same time, people get in the way and things slow down."

"Give me another example," Catherine prompted.

"We have a system for preventive maintenance," Peter stepped in. "We know the cycle times for everything from tires to light bulbs. Our preventive maintenance system lets us fix things in the shop rather than at the gate when a flight is about to take off. Our core function is *on-schedule.* The last thing we want is a flight delayed to replace a light bulb in the lavatory."

"Okay, one more level of work," Catherine announced. "Then we are going to call it a day."

Properties in Levels of Work						
Level of Work	Longest Time Span Goals	Typical Managerial Role	Function	Tools	Problem Solving	Value
S – IV	2-5y	Executive Manager Vice-Pres	Integrates multiple systems and subsystems	System metrics.	Systems Analysis	Multi-system efficiency, throughput.
S – III	1-2y	Manager	Creates system. Monitors system. Improves system.	Flowcharts, sequence, planning.	Root cause analysis, comparative analysis	Single system efficiency, consistency, predictability.
S – II	3-12m	Supervisor Project Manager Coordinator Project Engineer	Makes sure production gets done, implements the production system	Schedules, checklists, meetings.	Experience, manuals, best practices	Accurate, complete, on-time.
S – I	1d-3m	Production Technician Labor Clerical	Production	Real tools, equipment.	Trial and Error	Quality

"This is a tough one. Everything up to now has been fun," Javier described. "At the bottom three levels of work, the output is connected to the activity. You do something, you see something happen.

"But at level IV, you do something, you may not see the end result for 2-5 years. Guaranteed delayed gratification. And this level of work is not looking at just a single system, but multiple systems at the same time."

"Sounds like multi-tasking," Catherine observed.

"Hardly," Javier was quick to point out. "Humans can't multi-task, it's still one focused thing at a time. This level IV role looks at the dependency of one system on a second system, or the interdependency of three or more systems, or a contingency event from one system that may delay an event in another system, or troubleshooting bottlenecks in one system caused by an element in another system."

"Give me an example," Catherine nodded.

"Take our baggage system," Javier explained. "The sales department wanted revenue from checked bags, so they proposed an additional charge for checked luggage. Marketing resisted saying it would cut down our online bookings, because our business customers don't want to pay extra for luggage. Operations fought the baggage charge because they want as much of the luggage professionally loaded in the belly of the plane. They said when every passenger tries to put a roll-aboard in the overhead bin, it slows things down. Our customer experience department said our business customers don't want to check bags so they can avoid baggage claim. Competing systems all want something different. And making a decision one way, impacts the other systems."

"And?" Catherine furrowed her brow.

"Remember, it all started because sales wanted to increase revenue. Marketing was afraid it would make our customers consider another airline. Sales argued that we had the expense of baggage handling one way or the other and ultimately, the cost would go into the ticket price. Our fares are already marginally priced above our competition anyway. Of course, the competition covers the difference by charging for bags. Our marketing manager contended that our business customer is smart enough to see through our competitor's up-charge and that overall, our ticket was less expensive."

"So, what's the right answer?" Catherine asked.

"That's the thing. There are so many variables in the decision, we probably won't know for two or three years which logic will prevail in the marketplace. In the short term, some airlines make good money off their baggage fees, but in the long run, baggage fees may alienate their core customer. Our surveys tell us that our business customer hates getting nicked for bag fees. At one airline, if the customer doesn't check the bag at the time of reservation and shows up at the gate, it costs $100 to gate check. Our customers hate that."

"So, we are listening to surveys?" Catherine questioned.

"More than that," Javier continued. "The level IV manager has to pay close attention to every system. A ton of data is gathered and analyzed. Scenarios are constructed and feedback is collected from anyone who might understand a hidden variable."

"Sounds like groupthink?" Catherine prodded.

"Except for one thing. At the end of the day, the level IV manager is accountable for the decision. Data and input are part of the process, but the level IV manager is accountable."

Catherine was satisfied. Her executive team understood level of work. Even, Jim Dunbar, who sat in the back of the room, was proud of the thinking that started with the Culture Club. But, he was most proud that the Culture Club was no longer an outlier group.

Hierarchy

During the week since the last President's Meeting, each manager identified the level of work required in their department.

"Use the rule of necessity," Catherine admonished. "If it's not necessary, we don't do it. If it is necessary, we have to do it. Lots of things in lots of companies don't get done, because they are not made necessary. If we deem that something is necessary, then we have no choice, we have to do it. That goes with machinery and equipment. That goes with personnel."

Each manager brought their decisions to the meeting. Catherine required each manager to present their departmental structure to the rest of the team. Using level of work, the reports were similar, though the functions were completely different.

"So, here is my production team," Johnny began. "Each team member has a supervisor. I have three supervisors on my supervisor team. And I am the manager of the avionics division."

Johnny's Team		
Level of Work	Longest Time Span Goals	Avionics Division
III	1-2y	Manager
II	3-12m	Supervisor
I	1d-3m	Production Technician

"So," Catherine clarified. "Your production team reports to your supervisor team and your supervisor team reports to you?"

"No, my production team reports to people all over the company," Johnny flatly stated.

"But, you are the manager?" Catherine asked.

Mary jumped in. "Yes, Johnny is the manager. But, his team reports to the purchasing department for the parts they use. And the team reports to the Quality Control department related to performance standards."

"But, Johnny is the manager," Catherine protested.

"Yes, but he is not a manager so people can report to him," she insisted. "His team reports to lots of people in the company. It's not a matter of reporting. It's a matter of accountability. As the manager, Johnny is accountable for the output of his team. Which means, if his technicians get a parts order screwed up with purchasing, Johnny, as the manager, is accountable. If an equipment installation fails to meet quality standards, Johnny, as the manager, is accountable."

"This sounds like you have talked about this before," Catherine observed. "But I am curious. If a technician makes a mistake, why is Johnny the one accountable?"

"By definition, a manager is that person held accountable for the output of the team," Mary said.

"Okay. Perhaps I agree, but why?" Catherine challenged.

"Because Johnny controls the resources. We always assume the team member shows up to do their best."

"Yes, but a mistake is a mistake and, need I remind you, we are in the life and death business," Catherine was firm.

"But, Johnny, as the manager, selected the team member and assigned the task. As the manager, Johnny is in charge of technician training and practice. He controls the tools, sets the pace and determines the quality standard. Johnny controls all the resources, and is accountable for the output of his team."

Jim Dunbar beamed in the back of the room.

Peter dove in. "So, as we create these managerial relationships, it's not a reporting relationship, it's an accountability relationship. And, it's the manager accountable for the output of the team."

Peter's Team		
Level of work	Longest Time Span Goals	Maintenance Division
III	1-2y	Manager
II	3-12m	Supervisor
I	1d-3m	Production Technician

"Walk me through yours," Catherine directed.

"Mine looks almost identical," Peter said. "My maintenance technicians come to work every day. I expect each team member to bring their full attention and discretionary judgment to make decisions and solve problems. My supervisor team is accountable for scheduling all the resources necessary to match the production output, to keep our planes safe and on schedule. As the manager, I am accountable for creating the system in which all our maintenance is done. I constantly get feedback from my production teams and my supervisor team to modify the systems we created. At the end of the day, however, I am the one accountable for creating and maintaining the systems."

"Okay, got it," Catherine nodded. "And Frank, how about you?"

Frank's Team		
Level of work	Longest Time Span Goals	Flight Crew
III	1-2y	Manager
II	3-12m	Supervisor
I	1d-3m	Flight attendant Gate agent

"Same thing," Frank replied. "I am the manager of all flight crew personnel outside the cockpit, including gate agents. My team members work directly with the customer, doing their best to make everything happen on the ground and in the air. Each has a supervisor responsible for scheduling personnel for all of our flights. Our supervisor role is critical, high level II. Without the right personnel at the right gate at the right time, planes get delayed. A big part of the supervisor role is training. They are accountable to make sure everyone meets our training standards in safety, operations and emergency response. As the manager, I am accountable for creating the system to make all that happen. It took me two years to select and replace our old scheduling software with a new web-based system."

Catherine was impressed, but she wasn't finished. "Mary, you're last. Your role is a bit different. You are the manager of Frank, Peter and Johnny. What does your level of work chart look like?"

Properties in Level of Work				
Level of work	Longest Time Span Goals	Operations Division		
IV	2-5y	VP - Operations		
		Maintenance	Avionics	Flight Crew	Ground Crew
III	1-2y	Manager	Manager	Manager	Manager
II	3-12m	Supervisor	Supervisor	Supervisor	Supervisor
I	1d-3m	Production Technician	Production Technician	Flight Crew Gate Agents	Baggage, fuel, tugs

"My role is to integrate everything together," Mary replied. "Many companies talk about their departments as silos. They complain their departments don't communicate well and are rife with personality conflicts. It's my job to create harmony, to make sure all departments are working in concert, each optimized to the other with smooth transitions where work has to be coordinated. I was in on the discussion about whether we should charge for checked baggage."

"Sounds like you are the peace keeper. It must test your human relations skills," Catherine smiled.

"Yes, there are human relations skills required, but remember that most issues we face, as an organization, are structural issues. I can't solve those problems by being nice to people. Smile training doesn't work. The systems we create have to be the right systems. We have to clearly define the accountability and authority that goes with each role and each level of work. If we get the structure right, my life, as a manager is wonderful. If we get the structure wrong, my life, as a manager, is miserable, and no communication seminar or sensitivity training will fix a structural problem."

Catherine continued to smile and slowly nodded. She was learning this business fast. And she picked the right people to teach her.

With a Capital T

"We've got trouble," Catherine confided to Jim. "I have been going over the books. It didn't show up on the balance sheet or the income statement. I had to dig deeper into some of the supporting schedules. After that, I had to go back to the transaction level in our online bank statements for the detail."

Across the desk, Jim listened carefully. He used to sit on the other side, but now he was Chief Culture Officer, and Catherine was the CEO.

"Did you know, a majority of our topline does not come from passenger revenue miles? It comes from the government." Catherine looked him square, watching for a *tell*, a crack in the armor. Jim sensed this was not a casual question. Catherine was not looking for information. She was testing Jim's integrity.

"I knew we flew some unprofitable routes, more than a handful, but I didn't know what to make of it," Jim replied.

"We're on the dole," Catherine explained. "We are flying several routes almost empty. When I matched up the routes to revenue, it looked normal. When I matched up the routes to passengers, we came up empty. So I went to look where the revenue came from. It looked like a grant, or a stipend. Son of a bitch, we are on the government's payroll."

Jim was confused. "Why would we get money from the government for flying empty?"

"That's what I want to know. I asked our accounting department for the backup, a contract, a letter of agreement. I got nothing but shrugged shoulders. We get a direct deposit every month. It's automatically coded to an expense department. Remember, it's an expense department, but it turns 32 percent profit every month. So, it shows up as a negative expense, that's what caught my eye."

Jim was not an accountant, but he knew how to read an income statement. "You said this accounts for the biggest percentage of our revenue?"

"Yep," Catherine replied. "This airline is flying on fumes. But, that's not the worst of it. A year ago, we guaranteed some aircraft leases to a company called Hatchmeyer Leasing. Those leases are 20 percent above rate. Hatchmeyer Leasing is in receivership and the trustee just accelerated the note."

Jim was on high alert. "Orville Hatchmeyer was the legislator killed in the crash up in Dickinson. This doesn't smell right."

Catherine stared at Jim. "I know," she said. "There is a clause in the agreement that allows for the acceleration. It's almost like a pass-through to the lender. If Hatchmeyer Leasing defaults to the bank, our planes on the hook. Hatchmeyer is dead, we're on the hook."

"And?" Jim was curious.

"We can make the lease payments as long as we can operate, but we can't pay it all at once. We could surrender the planes, but then we can't operate."

"So, we're screwed?" Jim stated, in the form of a question.

"Not really," Catherine replied. "The last thing the lender wants is a used airplane. It's the trustee for Hatchmeyer that accelerated the note, not the lender."

"It still doesn't sound good," Jim observed.

"It's not good, but, it's not the end of the world," Catherine stopped. "But, it might be the end, when I cancel all the government contracts."

Why?

"Why would Catherine cancel all the government contracts?" Jim thought. It was an unspoken thought. But, spoken or not, Jim's face betrayed the question.

"Jim, this airline was built on integrity," Catherine was adamant. "On the wall, in our lobby, integrity is number one in our Values' Statement. We are taking government money to provide a service that is out of sync with integrity. We are stealing."

At first, Jim tried to argue. "I am sure there is a reasonable explanation," he floated.

"I would like to believe there is, but I can't find one," she rebutted. "On my desk are seventeen contracts, signed by Al Ripley that make no sense. Bridges to nowhere, except they are in the air."

"So, what are you going to do?"

"Twenty-four hour rule," Catherine replied. "I am going to sleep on it, not jump to any conclusions. Twenty-four hour rule."

Ethical Dilemma

"Are you out of your minds?" Al Ripley demanded. Coriolis headquarters sat adjacent to DFW airport, 558 nautical miles from Denver. Doug MacBride and the rest of the board listened to Ripley's explanation.

"You put this woman up there to run this airline, and she comes back with a cockamamie story about fraud. You fly me down here to haul my ass on the carpet. Look, you asked me to do a job. You put me up there to run this piss-ant airline with little regional routes, little bitty airplanes into little bitty towns. I showed you how to make money in losing markets, and you pulled me off the job. And now, you want to bust my balls."

"Calm down," Doug MacBride cautioned. "We just want your side of the story."

"Look, you are the board," Al Ripley pulled his jacket forward, as if the fight was over, "but you gave me a job to do. You wanted a return on your investment. I gave it to you."

"We just want your side," Doug repeated. "You know, I have been in your corner, all along. We had to pull you out of Outbound because of the plane crash. But, Catherine Nibali noticed some irregularities related to our contracts with the government. She wants to pull those contracts, this thing is about to go public. We need to know where we stand. We have a good legal team, but this story could go sideways fast."

"She can't pull those government contracts," Ripley objected. "We worked hard to put those deals together. I don't know what she has up her sleeve. Is she out to embarrass the entire company?"

"We're not sure about her motives," MacBride responded. "Quite frankly, we don't care about her motives. We have an investment in this company, an investment that hasn't paid off. Outbound showed promise in the beginning, but we have our doubts."

Ripley looked around the table. Doug MacBride, in his time of need, served him up as a sacrificial lamb. The board pulled him out of Outbound Air, but they did not leave him in the cold. Coriolis, as a company, lived up to its end of his employment contract.

"Look, you guys have been fair with me," Ripley began his appeal. "I know you needed to show remorse for the plane crash in Dickinson. I get it. But, if you put me back in the game, I can show you how to save face and turn this situation around. The NTSB will announce their findings soon. If the crash was going to take us down as an airline, we would already be on the ropes, but we are still in business. It is likely the NTSB will blame pilot error. We can survive that. But, if Nibali comes up with some allegations of fraud, frivolous as they may be, this whole venture could sink. Think about the impact to the portfolio."

Ripley was smooth and convincing. Each board member looked to the other for support. Non-verbal consensus was the goal. They might get there, but not today.

"Thank you for your time," MacBride broke the silence. "We will be in touch. If there is anything you think of, that might help guide us through this, please call me."

Ripley hoped to leave the meeting with more certainty. He hated limbo, but limbo ruled the day.

Corporate Response

"What did they say?" Jim wanted to know.

"The board is very disturbed," Catherine replied. "They are sending in a team from our legal department. Not sure if the board wants to know where we stand or if they want a cover-up."

"What's your next move?"

"I am looking at the termination clauses, to see what provisions exist, in the event we try to cancel the contracts. I don't know how this got approved on the government's side or what kind of penalties are in place in case we breach the agreement.

"A bigger problem is to determine what routes we have left that are profitable and which routes have potential. If we cancel these contracts, the pretense is gone. We have to become a real airline."

"What about the accelerated lease payments on the planes?"

"That one, I think I have worked out," Catherine disclosed. "I have a friend at the bank. We have to make a formal application, but I think we can pull the lease out of the receivership and go direct with the lender."

"Sounds complicated," Jim said.

"That's why they pay me the big bucks," Catherine chuckled. "Where are *those* decisions on your level of work chart?"

Legal

Down the hall from her office, Catherine entered the conference room. The chair at the head of the table was occupied. Leon Wolfe was a project manager in Coriolis' legal department.

"Welcome to Outbound," Catherine smiled. "Though, you could have saved yourself the trouble of a trip out here to Denver. As soon as I found the contracts, I emailed them up to Doug MacBride."

"Yes, Doug forwarded them to me. That's not why I am here. Until we determine the best course of action, no more emails on the subject. You can talk on the phone, but nothing in writing. This whole scenario is on lock down."

"Oh, really," Catherine mused. "And just exactly how do you intend to keep a lid on this thing?"

"I'm not," Leon replied. "You are. From this moment forward, mum's the word. You can discuss this with

Doug MacBride back in Dallas, but no internal discussions. No discussions with your staff. That's why I flew down here. Doug wanted to make sure you were clear on how to handle this."

"I am afraid you are a bit late," Catherine raised her eyebrows. "It took me a few days and a couple of people in accounting to do the research. My accounting department knows as much as I do about this."

Leon was quiet. He was thinking about damage control. "As far as I can tell, these are legitimate contracts with the government. There is nothing wrong with a legitimate contract. So, if your accounting people are too curious, please tell them not to worry. Tell them you are glad that everything checked out and there is no problem."

"And, what should I tell the press?"

"Press? What press? How did the press get tipped off to this?" Leon's eyes darted back and forth.

"They didn't," Catherine leaned in. "But you know, and I know, they will. At some point, there will be a knock on my door and a television camera in my face."

Limbo

"I don't know, Jim," Catherine confided. "I am a bit incensed that the board would send down a legal goon to instruct me on what I do and say, if even for a few days. I know we need to do some fact finding, figure out where we stand legally and do some analysis on the impact of the decision. But, this delay doesn't feel right. No one will fault me if I take my time, but time will run out. If I don't make the decision, right or wrong, someone else will make the decision for me."

"What do you think is on the table?" Jim asked.

"We're not even supposed to be discussing this," Catherine continued. "But I need to talk it out. Sometimes, I don't know exactly what I think, until I say it out loud. A brilliant thought, put into words, sometimes sounds really stupid."

"What do you think is on the table?" Jim repeated.

"They are going to cover it up. They will examine the contracts, declare nothing is illegal."

"Do you think something is illegal about the contracts?"

"Technically, no," Catherine replied, "but there is a smell to it."

"How so?"

"It's funny. I read some of the fine print. Since we are under contract with the government, we have to comply with specific wage and hour provisions at the federal level, including the way we manage our payroll in relationship to the union.

"You know me. It's important that our employees have input on many things about the way the company is run, but this union thing leaves too many opportunities for corruption. Anyone who works for us, has to belong to the union. Anyone who belongs to the union has an involuntary payroll deduction.

"And, guess what? The dates on the contracts are within two weeks of when the union successfully organized our employees. I don't like it."

"So, if the contracts are legal, but you don't like them, what's the alternative?" Jim asked.

"That's the problem," Catherine shook her head. "If I don't like the contracts, I can cancel them. But we built up a lot of overhead when Al Ripley was here. I don't know if we would survive without those contracts. Someone once told me, never shoot my camel in the desert."

"What do you think would happen?"

"In the short term, devastating. If we cancel the contracts, it's going to kill our cash flow, affect our relationship with the bank and give us less room to maneuver around the aircraft leases."

"And if we just keep going, keep things under our hat, what will happen?"

Catherine stopped to think. "Nothing. In the short term, nothing will happen. We can stay on the gravy train. We will have enough cash to negotiate with the lender on the leases. Nothing will happen."

"It's a tough decision. But, Ripley will say you don't have much of a choice."

Catherine's eyes focused. "It has been a very long time since I found myself in a position where I didn't have a choice."

Jim let the words sink in. "Okay. You have a choice, but the alternatives don't look good."

"In the short term." Catherine continued. "But you have to think what will happen over time. At some point, a reporter will start asking questions. And those questions are the same questions I am asking now. Sure, we can devise some spin response. We can say the contract was legal. We can challenge the reporter to find some evidence of corruption, or fraud. But, you know what? The reporter might find some evidence. I am not so sure, if *I* dig deeper, *I* might find it.

"Then where would we be? I do not want to sit in a board meeting and draw straws to determine the designated defendant who goes to prison. What support would we get from the bank at that point? How would our customers respond?

"And if we cancel the contracts and suffer the short term pain, we might lose some of what we take for granted. Since we bought the airline from you, have we ever been able to stand on our own two feet, without being propped up by some crony government contract? We might have to develop more discipline. We might have to rethink our systems. But, we will be a better airline for it."

"What latitude do you think the board will give you?" Jim was afraid he knew the answer.

"We are in Denver. The board is in Dallas. They do not make operating decisions, but they do select the CEO. So I have whatever latitude I want to take. But, at the pleasure of the board, I might lose my job."

A Wink and a Nod

"She wants to do what?" Al Ripley demanded. "I can't believe you guys would sit here and take this kind of insubordination from a rank amateur like Catherine Nibali."

"That's why we called you back in here," Doug MacBride defended. "This is an unusual situation. We have never had a decision like this before, and, quite frankly, it looks like you set this whole thing up. We are wondering, maybe, if you should be the one to go back and fix it."

There was complicit silence around the board room table.

"Now, let me get this fair and square," Ripley picked up the lead in the conversation. "You want me to go back into this firefight, relieve Nibali from her command and fix this thing, once and for all?"

Doug MacBride jumped in to temper the directive. "No, that's not what we are saying. We are saying that, perhaps, you could go to Denver, off the record, sit down and have a chat. You negotiated the contracts. You can likely explain why it makes sense to stay the course. I mean, our legal department reviewed the contracts, they were negotiated in good faith. No one was coerced. There was no bribe money paid under the table. It looks like a clean transaction.

"And, based on our analysis," Doug continued, "if we let go these contracts, it might jeopardize the whole Outbound operation. That is not what we paid Catherine Nibali to do. We put Kevin DuPont in, to stabilize the situation and Catherine to grow the business over the long haul."

"I want to understand this clearly," Ripley pressed. "If she has any notions about pursuing her strategy, am I clear to tell her to stand down?"

Doug MacBride let out an exasperated breath, but he was prepared for this clarification. "No," he said. "If Catherine is relieved of her duties as CEO, that will have to come from the board. But we think you are in a unique position to explain how the contracts were negotiated and why it is in our best interest to let them stand."

Ripley was already checking his cellphone for the next Outbound flight to Denver.

Flightplan

As Al Ripley passed through security in the Dallas airport, he noticed something different at the Outbound gate. He was greeted by the gate agent, "Good morning, Mr. Ripley."

"Good morning." Ripley looked around. "Where is everyone?"

"The plane checked in full, so we started boarding. We waited on you. Our Denver office sent word you would be flying with us today."

"My boarding pass says you have me in row 8. I hope you bumped someone out and saved me a seat in first-class," Ripley insisted.

"All of our seats are first class seats, Mr. Ripley, and we saved your seat in row 8. Our CEO, Ms. Nibali, said to give you our first class customer experience on your way to Denver."

Ripley scowled down the jetway.

"Good morning, Mr. Ripley," the pilot stepped out from behind the cockpit door. "We're glad you're here. It's a great day for flying."

"Good morning, Mr. Ripley, let me take your bags," chirped a stout flight attendant dressed in slacks and a polo shirt. "We're flying full today, but we have room right above your seat for your roll-aboard."

"You didn't save me a seat in first-class?" Ripley was irritated.

"All of our seats are first-class seats. I know you will be comfortable in row 8. Step lively, now. We're just closing the cabin door, ready for take-off."

Ripley spotted the empty seat in row 8. Outside, underneath the cockpit, the tug nudged forward, the plane shifted ever so slightly. The flight attendant smiled and Ripley moved quickly to his seat. "Is this any way to run an airline?" he thought to himself.

As he turned to sit, he noticed that even row 8 had plenty of leg room. It wasn't first-class, but it was comfortable. "Good morning, you must be Al Ripley," his seat mate leaned over. "I recognized you from the news clippings from a couple of years back. With all the fuss from the flight crew, we figured somebody important was holding up this flight." The inquisitor turned and buried his attention back to the newspaper displayed on his tablet.

The plane pushed back as the flight attendants completed their safety briefing. Ripley checked his watch. It was still five minutes to the official departure time, but they rolled from the gate for takeoff.

The climb out was a little bumpy, but the small jet headed quickly to altitude. Ripley looked around the cabin. Things had changed. Little things. He counted the rows, two short. No wonder he had leg room.

The flight attendants moved quickly through the cabin, distributing drinks and snacks. "Good morning, Mr. Ripley. And, good morning to you Mr. Perez. It's nice to see you again." The inquisitor looked up from his tablet with a smile. "Good morning, Joann. Yes, it's a great day to fly."

"Two creams in your coffee?"

"Yes, thank you," Perez replied.

"And Mr. Ripley, you didn't complete your profile before you checked in, so what would you like to drink today?"

"Sorry, I didn't know I had to fill out a profile," Ripley smirked.

"Not a problem, that's how we find out what you want to drink before you board."

Al Ripley was puzzled.

"You don't fly this airline much, do you?" Perez chuckled.

Ripley looked around. Oversized luggage compartments, universal power ports at every seat. This was not the airline Ripley left 12 months ago.

Faceoff

When Al Ripley arrived at Outbound's Denver office, Catherine Nibali was already seated at the head of the table in the conference room.

"Welcome," Catherine nodded. "Would you like some coffee?"

"Yes, please. Black, two sugars." Al Ripley cased the room. "Catherine. I believe you and I need to talk in private. I have instructions, directly from the board, that we are to have a confidential conversation. The board has a very direct message that I am to deliver, without interference. After we meet, we can decide who needs to know the content of our discussions."

"I am certain your message is quite confidential," Catherine smiled. "I know what it says about an organization where important things are only discussed behind closed doors. Please, proceed."

"The board is quite upset with your intentions to cancel our government contracts. Why, those contracts are our bread and butter. You see, Ms. Nibali, your problem is, you think you are in the airline business."

"You're right, I *do* believe we are in the airline business, and, I can see how you think that is a problem."

"Catherine, do you have any idea what will happen if you cancel those contracts? In 72 hours, we will be served notice of default."

"Oh, I am certain there will be some negotiation before we pull the plug, but I also understand how the general public feels about government waste. I don't think it will be that difficult to scuttle those contracts."

Ripley was not used to push back from someone he considered to be powerless against him. "And, Catherine, without those contracts, do you have any idea what would happen to your revenues in the next quarter?"

"Mr. Ripley, why did the board send you out here to talk to me?"

"I will tell you why," Ripley snapped. "You are the third CEO to sit in this office the past year. That doesn't look good in our portfolio. The board doesn't want to have to replace you. But, they gave me the nod. They know I put those contracts in place. They are aware of the revenue hit we would take if you move to cancel them. That's why they sent me. If you leave well-enough alone, you will likely keep your job. Otherwise, I believe you are looking at your successor."

"Well, Mr. Ripley," Catherine replied. "Here's what I know, based on the research and analysis of my team. The timing of the government contracts and the muscle from the unions occurred within two weeks of each other. Some could speculate, but, speculation aside, those government contracts tie up our resources in markets that will never grow. We can't put a plane in an emerging market, because our lending limits support planes in dead markets. The board hired me to grow this airline. When you were CEO, you grew revenues, you didn't grow an airline. You grew revenues on the back of the government and you tied up all our resources to do it. For every plane we fly empty on a government reimbursement, we lose the opportunity to fly the plane full in another market where we can grow."

"Ms. Nibali, while I took the trouble to travel out here and speak with you in person, my message is very short. Do not cancel those government contracts. If you do, there will be hell to pay, if you get my drift."

"Mr. Ripley, are you a member of the board?" Catherine replied with a question.

"Well, no, but I was sent here by the board."

"In that case, it is unlikely you have read my contract. It is not an unusual contract, but it does say that, should the board be unhappy with my performance, it is within their rights to terminate my employment. Which means, I serve at the pleasure of the board. If the board wanted to terminate my employment, they would have sent someone with the authority to do that."

First Move

Jim Dunbar was curious. The text on his phone pushed up the time for the President's Meeting.

"I'm glad you could all come on such short notice," Catherine said. "You know we constantly review our existing operations to make sure we make the best decisions. According to Javier's analysis, our efficiency ratios look pretty good. We've made great strides in the past few months." She stopped to survey the faces at the table. No one was buying her speech. The short notice of the meeting belied its importance. The group knew this meeting was not about efficiency ratios. Al Ripley just left the building. Jim Dunbar was waiting for Catherine to take the gloves off.

"But," Catherine continued calmly. The decision she was about to announce was made before Ripley showed up. "Our efficiency ratios work pretty well for our revenue structure. I am very pleased." Again, she paused. "The problem is, our efficiency ratios on passenger miles put us in last place in the industry.

"Everyone is working well within their own departments, but we need to look at our airline differently. Javier, I want you to head up a cross-functional team. I want you to apply our efficiency models not only to revenues and revenue miles, I want those models put up against our return on assets. I know you are in operations, but I want you to get with our accounting department. By tomorrow, I want to know your recommendations and by the next day, your plan to reorganize those routes. Meeting adjourned."

Jim Dunbar sat still while the team filed out. He could see the uncertainty on their faces, but he also knew that within a couple of days, the ambiguity would disappear.

"Well?" Jim asked.

Catherine raised her brow.

"That was a diagnostic question," Jim explained. "What happened with Ripley?"

"Smoke, mirrors and bit of puffery," she replied. "I have been very clear with the board about my intentions related to our government contracts. I think Al Ripley has the ear of the board, at least the ear of someone on the board. They're scared. This little airline acquisition has been a bit bumpy. Not what they expected. They hired me and now they are getting conservative."

"So, what did you make of the meeting?" Jim asked.

"Al Ripley was here to remind me of what's at stake," Catherine explained. "My decision was already made, but Ripley moved up the timetable. If I hesitate, the board will exercise control. And if I move now and fail, the board will likely terminate. And if I move now and succeed, it is still going to be difficult."

"How so?"

"In the short term, we will take a hit, a big hit, to our revenues. But, I think I can buy time with our lenders to redeploy our assets in better markets. You have to think about what can happen over time."

"So, what do you think you are going to do?"

"I am not thinking. My decision is already made."

The Lion's Den

It was drizzling when Catherine's plane landed in Dallas. Armed with the analysis from Javier's ad hoc research team, she asked for a meeting with the board. They agreed. Doug MacBride invited Al Ripley.

"I told you she was insubordinate," Ripley was revving up, waiting for Catherine to arrive. "She is going to come in here and act like a rebellious child. And you guys are going to sit here and take it. You are going to give her a pass and she is going to kill your investment."

This slate of board members formed eleven years ago. Historically, most decisions were unanimous, there was rarely confrontation. Al Ripley's presence made the room uncomfortable. Before the meeting, he was coached by Doug MacBride to remain calm, but that was counter to Ripley's natural style.

The chairman of the board was Samuel Pierce. He put Coriolis together, as an investment fund, some thirty years earlier. But, the best investments they made were those where they acquired controlling interest and provided philosophical direction. More active than passive. It was not unusual for the board to voice their opinion and they were rarely shy to make a necessary change.

But Samuel Pierce never liked Ripley. "We appreciate your opinion, Al, but remember that you were invited here as a guest. During the discussion this morning, we may call on you to clarify some of the circumstances. We will not, however, entertain disparaging opinions about other people in the room. Is that understood?"

Ripley was satisfied. He pushed the board to its boundary and now knew where the boundary was. "Of course, Sam. I am just here to help."

The door swung wide, interrupting the exchange, and Catherine entered the room. She smiled to the group, settled her attention on Al Ripley. She unpacked a thin set of reports on the conference room table, pulled out a pen and took the leather chair that was saved for her.

"I am glad you could meet with me on such short notice," she began. "I believe the nature of the decision on the table, and its risk, requires that each of you have a clear understanding of the moves I am about to make with Outbound Air."

"Sounds like you have already made your decision," Doug MacBride said. "We haven't even heard your proposal." He glanced at Ripley.

"Indeed, I have made my decision. I am here today, to give you context for it, explain the basis and get your help in some of the execution details."

"My dear, Catherine," Ripley jumped in. "You cannot possibly ask us to believe you have already made your decision. And, since *I* put those government contracts together, *you* can't possibly know all the background required."

"Please," Samuel Pierce interrupted. "I would like to hear from Ms. Nibali. Mr. Ripley, if we need your clarification, we will ask. For now, Ms. Nibali, you have the floor and our undivided attention."

Catherine pushed a copy of her analysis in front of each board member. Javier's team worked into the night to publish numbers related to their efficiency models and load factors. Catherine quickly moved the discussion from the subject of revenues to the subject of return on assets. She made a strong argument that their biggest constraint to growth was an asset problem.

"We can keep flying planes on these subsidized routes, but we will never get bigger," she explained.

"You hired me to grow this airline, not to be a baby-sitter."

Al Ripley was certain that Catherine would attempt a smear campaign against him and that she might even allege the notion of corruption. But, she stayed on track. Her argument was all about operations, numbers, capacity and scalability. In the end, she got some breathing room.

"Ms. Nibali, you are right to bring this to the board," Samuel Pierce said. "You are also correct, there is risk. But, it is not the custom of the board to micro-manage your operational decisions. You were hired to grow this airline, and that is what we are going to let you do. Please, utilize our corporate accounting department. Our VP of Finance should be able to help you renegotiate those aircraft leases.

"Ms. Nibali, you have two quarters to show progress," Pierce concluded. "We will see you here in six months to see how you have done."

Al Ripley was furious, but kept his anger to himself. As Catherine said her good-byes, he even stood to shake her hand. He was the perfect passive-aggressive.

For Catherine, it was a long flight back to Denver.

Take a Deep Breath

The bank was next. Catherine and Jim pulled into the parking garage near the elevators. "A lot depends on our ability to pull this off," Catherine confided. "The board gave me some slack, but the bank has its regulators. If we cancel the government contracts, we will immediately go out of covenant with our leases. We may not have to report until the beginning of next quarter, but they will eventually find out. Better to prepare them in advance. If we are out of covenant, they can immediately call the leases and bring us down."

Jim nodded in agreement.

Into the Shark Tank

Catherine and Jim were greeted cordially enough. "Would you like some coffee while you wait? Mr. Sullivan and Mr. Hammermill will be with you in a moment."

Roger Sullivan was assigned to Outbound when Al Ripley took the reins. He was pleased to see the stability that the government contracts brought to the airline as it made its transition from prop aircraft to a fleet of jets. At times, he was concerned about the fleet, but Ripley earned his confidence. The revenue numbers didn't lie.

"Good morning, Ms. Nibali. And you must be Jim Dunbar," he said. "And, Mr. Dunbar, I believe you already know Mike Hammermill, from our Special Assets department."

Jim was only slightly stunned as he shook hands. "Hi, Mike. I didn't realize you worked here." It was like seeing a cop in the rear view mirror with blue lights flashing. What had Jim done wrong to be sitting across the table, again, from Mike Hammermill?

"It has been a while," Mike smiled. "Yes, I moved over here several years ago, right after we restricted your line of credit at First Bank. Roger dropped your file on my desk yesterday and asked if I would sit in. Don't worry, you're not in workout. Actually, I am here to keep you *out* of my department. You know, the regulators make most of our loan decisions. Right, now, you are okay."

"If you looked at the file, you might see that I sold the company a couple of years ago. I am only here as an observer. Catherine Nibali is the new CEO, so she is the one you are going to keep out of hot water."

"I saw that," Mike replied. "But I also know you are still involved in management. I admire your tenacity. When we pulled your line of credit, back at First Bank, most companies would have folded, but you stuck to it. Outbound Air is still alive."

"That is what we are here to talk about," Catherine jumped in. "Outbound is still alive, but it's not growing. And, it's not growing because we have a capital asset problem."

Roger Sullivan leaned forward. "That's what you communicated on the phone. That's why I brought Mike in. He knows the limits of our position. Like he said, it's pretty cut and dried. I hope you are not here looking for more capital. We reviewed your financial statements, and, while you are profitable, your return on assets are somewhat anemic. We can look at the public airlines and based on comps, you are already at your lending limits. We can't extend any more beyond the leases you already have."

"That's not why we are here," Catherine interrupted. "We don't need more money. But we are about to make a substantive change in some of our contracts. It might put us temporarily out of covenant. In our reporting cycle, you wouldn't find out for ninety days and that's only if you read the footnotes. I may need more than ninety days. That's why we are here."

Mike Hammermill closed the file folder, put his hands together and furrowed his brow. "Tell me more," he said.

"You are aware that a material portion of our revenue comes from government contracts that fly underserved routes. Those routes are underserved for a reason. There isn't enough market demand to justify the capital commitment. This means, those routes will only bring in the face amount of the contract. Those routes will never grow."

It was Roger's turn to interject. "I remember when Al Ripley negotiated those contracts, it wasn't that long ago. We ran the numbers together to floor plan those routes. You operate a small regional airline, but it's still all about numbers and capacity. Your break-even load factors run about 66 percent, give or take fuel costs. When we ran the numbers, we agreed the subsidies on those contracts had to account, not only for empty seats, but the add-on revenue lost from bags. Empty seats don't pay bag fees."

"Bags don't matter," Catherine said. "We eliminated bag fees."

There was a slight pause in Roger's cadence. "That's unfortunate, bag fees are very profitable. Any airline that charges bag fees will never give up that revenue line."

"Exactly why we did. We knew no other airline would follow."

"Well," he shook his head. "With the subsidies, all you have to do is sell another two dozen seats and you come out a winner."

"There aren't another two dozen seats in the market," Catherine replied. "That's why we are cancelling the contracts."

"I don't think you can do that," Roger chided. "Besides, instead of selling two dozen seats, you now have to get to your break-even load factors. And if you can't even sell two dozen seats, how are you going to make it?"

"I want to move those aircraft to other markets, markets with more potential," Catherine flatly stated.

Roger's face showed trouble.

But Jim Dunbar watched Mike Hammermill.

"How many markets?" Mike asked. Roger twisted his head around.

"Eight markets altogether," Catherine replied. "We have ten subsidized routes, but two are showing profitable with passenger revenue miles. So, we want to move eight."

"How fast can you meet your load factors?"

Catherine opened up her satchel and slid Javier's analysis across the table. The meeting continued for another twenty minutes.

"The bank can't give you permission to go outside your covenants," Mike concluded. "But, I can tell you when the regulators will come down hard on me and when I have to come down hard on you."

There was silence in the room.

"I just wanted you to know," Catherine confided. "I have a rule. No surprises."

"And, so, we know," Mike nodded. "You have to decide if you are willing to take the chance. I sit across the table every day from entrepreneurs with clouded judgment. Some make it, most don't. If you plan to cancel these contracts, and you go out of covenant next quarter, you will only have ninety days to cure. The regulators will make us reclassify the loan. That's it."

Back to Work

"I don't know," Javier pushed back. He was standing in Outbound's conference room with Catherine and Jim. "Just to handle the logistics, we may have to create a whole new department to shut down those contracts."

"And?" Catherine asked.

"We spent so much time and energy to define the core function and support functions in our company structure. We figured out the level of work required in each function, then we converted that into specific roles. We defined the management required, put names to faces and here we are.

"You are asking us to terminate contracts, close gates, move people around. We had it all organized, now you want us to disorganize. I think we are good at building, not so good at tearing things down."

"So, what's the difference between building up a new route and taking one apart?" Catherine pressed.

"Building something makes sense, it's functional, it's operational. Taking something apart, hopefully, is only temporary. It will need a team, but it's more like a project, something that has an end date. Then, what do we do with the department?"

"Exactly. It's a project," Catherine explained. "Canceling these contracts, shutting down gates and routes will be tricky. It's going to require cooperation from a bunch of departments. There are contractual things we need from legal, logistics from operations, public relations from marketing and to keep track of the costs, you need accounting support."

"Me?" Javier deflected. "I will need a whole staff to do all that work."

"That's why I picked you," Catherine smiled. "And since this is a temporary project, you don't get a staff to work with, you will have to borrow people and create a temporary team."

Javier continued to push back. "But, we took so much care to make sure everyone understood their role and the role of their manager. We know who is accountable and the authority that goes with it. And, now, you are asking me to disrupt all that, go across lines of authority, break up existing teams, and assign tasks to people who don't report to me. I know we need to get this job done, but I think we are going to create a lot of chaos."

Catherine smiled. "How so?"

"Look, I have seen this before. If I pull somebody off of a team, to work part time on my project team, it's like the person will have two managers. Their manager will assign tasks and I will assign tasks. We are going to make the person schizophrenic."

"So, before you borrow someone off another team, who should you check with?"

Javier knew Catherine was leading him down a path, and he was scurrying to keep up with her train of thought. "Well, I would need to check with that person's manager," he replied.

"And what would you negotiate with that person's manager?" she continued.

"How much time I need that person, what I need that person to do, anticipate conflicts with other responsibilities," Javier's mind was racing.

"And will you have the authority to make task assignments to this project team member?"

"Of course, I will have to be able to do that, to get the project done."

"But will you become this person's manager?" Catherine asked.

Javier stopped. "I will be able to assign tasks, but I will not be that person's manager. I will not conduct a performance review. I will not recommend changes in compensation."

"And, if this person on your project team underperforms, what will you do?"

Javier chuckled at the question. "I will go back to their manager and ask for someone else."

"So, you have a project, you are the project leader. As project leader, you need to borrow someone. You need a specific skill or service from another department. You go to the department manager and ask to borrow someone with that specific skill for a certain number of hours for a defined duration of time. And, you are NOT that person's manager."

"When you explain it like that, it doesn't sound so chaotic," Javier nodded.

"You're right, it's not chaos, because we established the specific (limited) accountability and the specific (limited) authority required to get the work done on your project. And if there is a priority or performance conflict, you know exactly who to talk to."

Javier was thinking while Catherine continued. "This happens all the time," she said. "You pulled together a cross-functional team when you prepared the analysis I used at the board meeting. That's why I always laugh when a manager says they have direct reports. The reality is, people report to people all over the organization. They can only have *one* manager, but they report to many different people. The problem is that we don't sit down and specifically define the accountability and authority that goes along with it.

"We spend a great deal of time defining how managers relate to their team members, but work gets done horizontally across the organization." Catherine stopped to look directly at Javier. "Lots of people work with, and are accountable to, other people who are not their manager. And when we don't define the specific (limited) accountability and the specific (limited) authority, people make stuff up and that's where trouble begins.

"So, yes, this is a big project, and to pull it off effectively will require a lot of cross-functional working relationships."

"This sounds like it is going to get complicated," Javier flatly stated.

"It would be complicated, but there are only seven cross-functional working relationships," Catherine explained. "Get with Jim and he will explain."

Chink in the Armor?

Al Ripley calmed down, but he knew his window to regain control of Outbound Air was closing. He wasn't sure why he wanted it back. His personal financial windfall stopped when Kevin DuPont took over as CEO. And it was unlikely that he could re-establish his slush fund bonus from the government contracts. There was too much scrutiny, now.

Even still, Ripley was competitive and he did not like to lose. While much about Outbound had changed, there was one remaining element that might prove fatal for Catherine Nibali.

Call to Arms

"Good afternoon," Ripley began. It only took one phone call to the union to set a meeting. Behind the scenes, a strategy committee always worked to make sure the union retained its position for collective bargaining and its position to collect dues.

"You are aware," Ripley continued, "that the new CEO at Outbound is making changes. These changes, I am afraid, are connected to the union's position at the airline."

Franz Weber and Adam Spader listened with concern. They ran the administrative section of the union that, two years earlier, managed to gain footing at Outbound. "But, I thought we had a back-scratch deal," Spader said. "The politicians keep pressure on the airline, the union funnels campaign contributions to the politicians. The airline gets government subsidies. What could go wrong?"

"The CEO is cancelling the government contracts. The subsidies will stop. It is only a matter of time before this thing unravels," Ripley explained.

"Why would they do that?" Spader asked. "Do they have a corporate death wish? It's a sweetheart deal, all above board and perfectly legal. I don't get it. Why would they bite the hand that feeds them?"

"I can't explain it," Ripley replied. "But if you want to put an end to it, you need to do some organizing. I think some strategically placed, small demonstrations in front of the media would go a long way to derailing her plans. Just as a matter of tactics, don't worry about some long term drawn out protest. She only has six months to turn the corner, or she's done."

"And, what happens then?" Spader wanted to know.

"I believe that I am successor to the position. The board has a fiduciary responsibility to its stockholders. Things ran well when I was there before. I see no reason why the board wouldn't reinstate me."

Grand Plans

Javier was already in the conference room when Catherine and Jim appeared. "Okay, I just want to review my plans for the project to shut down some of our gates and establish new routes for our idle aircraft," he said. "I divided things into six Key Areas and I have a project champion in each area. They each have their goals coordinated on a master plan that I control. It's a big project, but I selected a great team from all over the company to carry the load."

"All right, then, let's have a look," Catherine replied, sitting up to take a peek at the org chart Javier laid on the table.

"On this project, as a team, everyone has to work together," Javier explained. "People have certain limited authority and specific accountability. No one on the project is the manager of anyone else on the project."

"If no one is the manager, how will they know how to work together?" Catherine prompted.

"If we don't define the authority and accountability, people will make up their own rules. I thought this was going to be complicated, but you said there were only seven cross-functional working relationships. You told me to get with Jim. We looked at his list and here is what we came up with.

Cross-fuctional Working Relationships

- Service getting (service giving)
- Prescribing
- Audit
- Monitor
- Coordinate
- Collateral
- Advisor

Service Getting (Giving)

"How did you explain it to the team?" Catherine asked.

"As I approached each department manager, I told them I was working on a project, Project X, where I needed specialized resources from other departments. I explained what I needed, how much I needed and asked for their recommendation.

"For the project accounting, I asked our CFO for a controller level person with ten hours a week to track the direct and indirect costs for the project. The CFO suggested this would be a subsidiary ledger inside our accounting system anyway, and she assigned someone to the project.

"That's the way it went with the other five departments working on the project." Javier stopped because he knew that Catherine would have a question.

Javier Project Leader		<<Service Giving – CFO assigns Controller to work on project.	CFO
	<<Service Getting – Javier receives 10 hours of Controller time to work on project.		

Prescribing

"And what will *your* relationship be with each person working on your project team?" she asked.

"First, I am not the manager of the people on my project team," Javier was clear. "But, I do have authority to directly make task assignments within the scope of the project and within the parameters I negotiated with their manager. If there is a priority conflict between my task assignments and their manager's task assignments, the project team member just raises their hand. It's up to me and their manager to work it out between the two of us. We understand the context of their regular assignments and the context of the project work. The team member does not have to be schizophrenic, or play favorites, they just have to raise their hand."

	<<Service Getting	<<Service Giving	CFO Manager
Javier Project Leader			
	Prescribing >> Assigns task to Controller		Controller

"Okay, and what else?" Catherine asked.

Auditor

"We have some contractual commitments still in force. While we may renegotiate some of these obligations, until then, we have to abide by the contract. In some cases, I enlisted people to review the way we are shutting down some of the routes and gates. If we are about to do something that will put us in default, they can delay or stop what we are doing?"

"So, are they prescribing things for people to do, as a project leader?"

"No," Javier replied. "They are there to observe and review, but they do have the authority to delay or stop anything that jeopardizes the project.

"An auditor is like a safety director. The safety director doesn't tell people what to do, or give people task assignments. But, if someone is engaged in an unsafe work practice, the safety director has the authority to delay or stop the unsafe work practice, even though they are not anyone's manager."

"Okay, I get it," Catherine agreed.

Javier Project Leader	<<Auditor Authority to observe, stop or delay project	Auditor

Monitor

"And for some cases, I don't think we need a full blown auditor, but we may need someone to monitor the way we do something. The monitor and the auditor are looking for the same things, but the monitor does not have the authority to delay or stop the activity, only the accountability to report to someone who does have that authority. With this distinction, I can specifically assign the authority that is appropriate. Everyone understands, so no one gets bent out of shape."

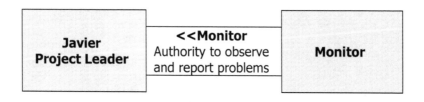

Javier Project Leader	<<Monitor Authority to observe and report problems	Monitor

Coordinating

"And what's this between marketing and operations?" Catherine asked.

"The timing is tricky," Javier explained. "We need to close a gate and shut down operations, but we also need to maintain confidence from our customer base. We need to communicate that we know what we are doing, and that we stand behind our commitments. At the end of the day, each ticket we issue is a contract for carriage, and we have to make that commitment good. Flight operations can decide what to do, but we have to coordinate with marketing to make sure we explain things accurately and timely to the public.

"So, I got my flight operations manager and my marketing manager together to explain their accountability. Funny, they both complained that they could not be accountable because they had to depend on the other manager to execute. I agreed that, yes, they had to depend on each other to effectively execute. If either called a coordinating meeting, the other person was required to attend and actively participate. Neither was each other's manager, but, both required to be responsive to each other."

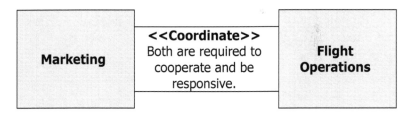

| Marketing | <<Coordinate>> Both are required to cooperate and be responsive. | Flight Operations |

Collateral

"And, what is this collateral relationship?"

Javier nodded. "It's like a coordinating relationship, but typically between project team members. They are required to cooperate, support and help each other. Where they have a priority conflict, they have to decide how their manager would handle the priority. If they can't figure it out, they have to ask their manager. In some cases, the manager has to step in, but if the team members can make the appropriate judgment, it speeds things along."

Manager		
Team Member	**<<Collateral>>** Both are required to cooperate and solve problems as their manager would solve them.	**Team Member**

Advisor

"And this advisor relationship?"

Javier stopped, looked first at Catherine and then at Jim. "That's easy," he concluded. "Jim is your advisor. He doesn't make task assignments. He doesn't audit or monitor, but when asked, he gives you his best judgment, advice and counsel."

Catherine	<<Advisor	Jim

Jim laughed. As the Chief Culture Officer, this had, indeed, been his role for a very long time.

The Resistance

Javier had eight gates to shut down. Though he renegotiated and terminated the government contracts, two routes would survive. There were legal snares, but, surprisingly little official resistance to suspending most of the provisions of the contracts.

It was the unofficial resistance that caught Javier off guard.

"Catherine, I think we have a problem," he explained. "We took down our signage and worked with our gate agents to relocate them to other hubs, but then this television reporter showed up. He wanted to know our reaction to the demonstration outside the terminal building."

"What did you tell him?" Catherine was not amused.

"I told him we were not aware of any demonstrations, so he took me outside. There were about a dozen people standing around, but as soon as I showed up and the TV camera turned on, they circled up and started chanting. Some of the faces looked familiar, but I don't believe any were Outbound employees."

"How long did this go on?" Catherine asked.

"Only about ten minutes. As soon as the TV reporter wrapped, everyone left, but I think it's going to hit the evening news."

Words of Warning

"Are you watching, this on TV, Doug?" Al Ripley breathed into the phone.

"Yes, I am watching," Doug MacBride said. "I don't know how to react. You warned us this would not be easy. I am sure the rest of the board is watching, too."

"If she just stayed the course, this would not be happening," Ripley boasted. "Just make sure when the board kicks Catherine to the curb, they remember that I am the one who took that pint-size little airline and built it. I know where all the skeletons are located. Don't let them waste much more time. She is going to destroy your investment, mark my words."

"Settle down, Al. The board is giving her more rope than I would have. We have to see if she can pull this off or if the rope is just there for a hanging."

"You know patience is not my strong suit," Ripley pressed. "I have been on the inside of this company. I know the internal politics. Catherine is trying to paint a rosy picture, like she has everything under control. But, I know better. She is stoking the fire against her employees and it's going to get worse. It wouldn't surprise me to see coordinated strikes across *all* of our gates. And, once it starts, she will have no way to stop it. I am your only hope. You put me back in as CEO and all this will go away in less than a half hour."

MacBride was quiet on the other end of the line.

"You still there, Doug?"

"Yes, yes, I am still here. If I have any word from the board, I will let you know."

All a Twitter

"Our Twitter feed has gone nuts," Mary announced to her table in the coffee room. "Our customer service department knows how to handle lost bags and delayed flights, but this is a little out of our league."

Javier joined her. "We had very detailed plans to shut down these gates, but I never anticipated that we would draw this much attention. Outbound had 45 seconds on CNN."

Mary was trying to think and when she wanted to think, she liked to draw diagrams. But the whiteboards moved to the conference room long ago. "Come on, let's go where I can think," she said, grabbing her things.

The door was open when they arrived. Inside, Catherine and Jim were deep in discussion. "Come on in," Catherine invited. "We could use some more heads on this." As Mary and Javier sat down, they were joined by Peter, Frank and Johnny, as well as two teammates from customer service and three people from marketing and social media.

"Let's start with what we know," Catherine took control. "I only want to hear facts. No opinions, no rumors, no solutions. Johnny, you take the white board and write this stuff down."

"We were in the middle of shutting down the first gate," Javier described. "All the other gates are still operating. This gate has no reservations for the next week and flew empty three times last week. That's why we picked this gate first."

"From marketing. Have we made any announcements, press releases, what have we made public?" Catherine asked.

"We pulled the destination off published schedules and our website," Mary responded, "so, now, no one can book future reservations. We sent out 37 individual emails to people who purchased tickets. We apologized for the cancellations, refunded their money and offered a $100 voucher for a future reservation. We made phone calls to those affected who are in our frequent flyer program. I mean, with 37 bookings, it was pretty manageable."

"But, nothing published to the public?" Catherine confirmed.

"Not yet. I mean, we have a press release ready to go. That's why I am so surprised by our Twitter feed. We have more negative comments on Twitter than we have affected passengers."

"And, the news story on TV?" Catherine pressed. "How did the networks find out we even did this?"

Javier stepped in. "The reporter that I talked to, said he got a phone call and so they showed up. A dozen or so people with cardboard signs, chanting about ruthless corporate greed. And as soon as the cameras turned off, they all left. But when you look at the news story, you would have thought there were hundreds of people holding vigils into the night."

As the facts were recorded onto the white board, Catherine's eyes began to narrow. She didn't like it, but she was putting a plan together. Twenty minutes into the discussion, she declared the first moves.

"Jim and I have been working on the announcement of our expansion into eight new markets. That's the lead. Mary, get with marketing and make it look bold on the home page of our website. I want monitors on all of our social media pages. Respond to every negative post. Write a one sentence personal apology and put a link to the announcement about our new markets."

"Do you want me to arrange for a press conference," Mary asked.

"No, let's wait. We have only been on TV once and by the time tomorrow gets here, it might be buried in the news cycle. Who watches TV news, anyway? Mary, I need your department to write some talking points based on the landing page on our website. I want this out to every employee."

"If our employees are contacted by the media, who is our point person? Who should we direct them to, for comment? Do you want to handle all those requests?"

Catherine tilted back to look at the ceiling, as if the answer was there. "No," she replied. "Make sure we get those talking points out there. Any employee who is contacted by the media has my permission to speak for the company. Any employee who is contacted on social media has my permission to speak freely and respond to any question."

"Are you sure," Mary challenged. "Isn't that a little risky?"

"Everybody listen up," Catherine said. "Right now, things look messy and it appears that our internal morale is on the ropes. I don't believe it for a minute. Something is going on here, but it's not coming from inside this company. If there is anything I trust, it's our people. We are not going to win this skirmish with a politically correct press release. We are not going to win by spinning this story. We are going to win with our people. We are going to win with our culture. Someone is running a strategy against us and I want them to know that culture eats strategy for breakfast."

There was a knock at the open door. "Catherine, there is a call holding for you, a Mr. Hammermill. I told him you were in a meeting. He said he would hold. I told him it might be a long meeting. He still said he would hold."

The Rules

"Thank you for waiting, Mr. Hammermill, I just had to step out of my meeting. I can guess the reason for your call."

"Ms. Nibali. First I want to say, I admire your guts. Most people would take the easy way out. I have known Jim Dunbar for a long time and I see the two of you were cut from the same cloth. You know the risk and I commend you for your courage.

"But I want to tell you a baseball story. If the pitcher throws a fat pitch, and the hitter connects, sends a ground ball to the shortstop. And if that shortstop fields the ball and throws it to first base. And if first base steps on the bag and catches the ball before the runner gets there, the runner is out."

"Yes, Mr. Hammermill, the runner is out," Catherine confirmed.

"I just want to make sure you know the rules," he replied.

"Yes, Mr. Hammermill, everyone knows the rules."

"One last thing, Ms. Nibali."

"Yes, Mr. Hammermill."

"Run like hell. If you get to first base, I can get you to second base."

No News is Good News

The first story on CNN was the only time Outbound was mentioned in the news that week. The flurry on Twitter was short-lived. As Catherine suspected, no one really cared. Except Al Ripley. Instead of damage control, the management team focused on the redeployment of aircraft to increase flight frequency on existing routes and step into two new markets. Six more markets were planned after that.

Catherine knew the fight would not be won by damage control, but only by opening those new routes. She had to convince the board and she had to convince the bank.

Fly Full

Javier added an analyst to the marketing team. Outbound was a small airline, flying mostly regional jets, now. They abandoned the truly marginal markets leaving competitors to fly passenger prop planes. The regional fleet was fast and quiet. Each departure only had to fill seventy seats to fly full. The target market was the business traveler who was willing to pay just a little bit extra to be comfortable. Profit margins were not made by squeezing services. It was all about flying full.

There was just enough controlled chaos during the transition to keep everyone on their toes. The grand opening of every new gate was parlayed to reinforce all of the existing routes. Outbound penetrated its niche just outside every major market in the west.

Even still, travel habits die slowly. Catherine knew she had only a short time to complete this transition, not just to put airplanes in new markets, but to attract enough passengers to prove the route. There was no more safety net from government contracts to erase the red ink.

Catherine created key performance indicators and sent out reports as a daily flash. The most important indicator was the ratio between passenger revenue miles and capacity. She had accounting change the name of the computer report to "Butts in Seats."

After three days, Catherine realized this was not just a management report, this was a war cry. "The number is 100 percent," she announced. "I want the daily percentage posted system wide. I want it on every gate agent computer screen. I want every baggage handler to know. And I want them to know it every day."

Checkpoint

Three months passed. Catherine arrived in Dallas to meet with the board. She closed the door behind her, stacking her presentation materials at the end of the table. She was early and the board room had an eerie feeling about it. Her report to the board was only two pages, a balance sheet and a summarized income statement. In the corner of the room was a coffee service. Steam drifted from the fresh brew. The room was quiet.

Doug MacBride entered first. "Good morning, Catherine," he said. "I asked the rest of the board to delay their arrival by fifteen minutes, so I could have a word with you."

Catherine shifted in her chair. "Yes?"

"It has been three months since our last meeting. The board agreed to give you six months for this transition, so there is only one quarter to go. We already have the preliminary numbers and I have to tell you that we are not impressed. Before you moved the aircraft, at least we broke even on those marginal routes. Now, every new route is bleeding."

"Thank you for your concern," Catherine replied. "I am glad you are tracking my numbers and taking this as seriously as I am."

Doug expected a softer response, perhaps an apology. "Catherine, I know you have high confidence in your plan, but the board was approached by Al Ripley, and, I will be honest with you. Everything that Al Ripley warned us about, the way you are running things, has come true. Now Mr. Ripley can't be with us today, but he has the ear of the board. I don't think they will pull the rug out from under you at this meeting. They will be good to their word on the six month transition, but I want you to understand how serious this is. I want you to understand the board may have to make a tough decision."

"I understand the board's concern," Catherine nodded. "Is there anything else?"

"Yes," Doug paused. "I just want to mentally prepare you. If the board decides, the change will come quickly. It is highly likely that they will reinstate Al Ripley to succeed you."

The board meeting was not a reprimand. Cordial, but firm. Catherine reviewed the numbers. There were few questions. She talked mostly about marketing and promotion, market stats, load factors and competition. As Catherine stepped on the next Outbound flight back to Denver, she looked around the passenger cabin and smiled. The flight was full. Still plenty of legroom, but full. Ninety days to go.

Price Wars

And those days went quickly. Outbound Air was making headway. Feeling better, Catherine convened the President's Meeting in the conference room.

"We have some competition," Javier announced. "Joan, from marketing, picked up some chatter on the internet and today it was announced." All eyes moved from Javier to Joan. It was her first time in the President's Meeting, and she had troubling news.

"Go ahead, Joan," Catherine prompted. "Just tell us what you know. Don't sugarcoat it. We need the truth."

"Well," Joan cleared her throat. "We inched down our airfare, based on a formula tied to our cost basis. We haven't been digging into our profit, but as our costs came down, we adjusted the price, hoping to draw more passengers, so we could fly full."

"And?"

"And, we hit the radar. With the merger of US Air and American on the heels of Continental and United, there is a new consolidator buying gates out of Dallas. They have big planes and they are trying to kill our Dallas to Denver route. TransPac is the new name. Today they announced a $79 one-way fare. In less than 24 hours, we got a 12 percent cancellation rate on that route."

"I see," Catherine replied. "I heard about this merger." She leaned back in her chair. "I want all the facts. Who, what, where and why? We meet at 2:00 this afternoon. I want alternatives. Get with your teams and then report back here."

In the afternoon, there were facts and figures. Because TransPac was a public airline, most of their operating data was available. Javier's team used some proprietary cost calculators to estimate their cost structure.

"The $79 fare is slightly below their operating cost, not including overhead." Javier explained. "Unfortunately, they are flying 143 seats to our 70 seats. So while our per-hour operating costs are lower, our per-passenger cost is higher."

"Drop our fare to $69 and let's see their next move," Catherine said. "They are too big, too much overhead. They are already below cost. They won't follow. Get that pricing up on the website and out through our marketing channels."

The meeting adjourned. Jim Dunbar stayed behind. "How are we doing?" he asked.

"I am determined," Catherine replied. She then went quiet. "But, you know, we're not going to make it by the deadline. No amount of optimism will make the numbers magically appear. I am worried about the board and I am worried about the bank."

"What are you going to do?" Jim wanted to know.

"I am going to do what every entrepreneur would do," she paused. "I am going to ask for an extension."

Message to the World

Across the street from Outbound's Denver office, Catherine looked up at a fresh billboard staring down. Two men on a ladder pulled a new banner across, covering the old sign for a local restaurant.

---ANNOUNCING, the largest airline in the continental United States. TRANSPAC. BIG airplanes, LOW fares. Dallas to Denver - $59! ---

"Well, that didn't take long, and right across the street from our headquarters," Catherine told the group assembled in the conference room.

"What do we do now?" Mary asked.

"This is not forever," Catherine replied. "Transpac can't sustain this anymore than we can. The next plane that goes out, any seats that are left, the fare is $49. That's our next move. How long before we can get that pricing out?"

Hours clicked by.

An icon popped up on Catherine's email. "They went to $39," was the message from Javier.

"Okay, strap in," Catherine said out loud, though no one else was in the room.

The marketing department brought some make-shift lighting into the conference room. Catherine sat behind a desktop aircraft model of an Outbound plane.

"Let's see if we get this in one take," Catherine encouraged the amateur television crew. Mary made sure the microphone worked. Johnny set up the webcam.

Catherine started the video by describing the short history of Outbound Air, from prop planes to small passenger jets. Ten seconds later, she talked about competition and pricing. She named Transpac and stepped through the past three days of price wars. "This morning, Transpac responded to our $49 fare with their $39 fare." Her eyes now focused, searing the camera lens, addressing her next sentence to Transpac. "You want to play? I just authorized the next Dallas to Denver flight will have a fare of $19. And, Transpac, I just want to put you on notice. The next departure, we are going to fly for free."

Nice to Be Small

When the team assembled the video shoot, they were not sure what to expect, but, whatever it was, they did not expect Catherine to offer to fly free. A half hour later, Joan, from marketing leaned against the inside of Catherine's office door. "You should see our Twitter feed," she said.

Catherine twirled around in her chair. She was staring out the window toward the billboard across the street. "Their $39 fare is still posted up there," she replied. "I don't think they are going to match our $19 fare. So, what's this about our Twitter feed?"

"You created quite the buzz," Joan nodded.

"No, *we* created quite the buzz," Catherine raised her eyebrows. "I said the words, but you guys made it happen."

"It's still quite the buzz. But, that's not the interesting part. Our reservations are up seven percent, hour over hour, on our full fares. We followed your instructions, the $49 fare already landed in Denver, our $19 fare is boarding right now, and our free flight cues up first thing tomorrow morning. Then we're back to full fare."

"And what does a national television spot cost?" Catherine asked.

Joan just smiled. "I get it," she replied.

The Extension

Catherine and Jim waited for Mike Hammermill to join them. Catherine set this appointment three months ago, to meet in person. She hoped this would be a celebration, but it was not to be. The bank's conference room was a stark contrast to the war room at Outbound. Sterile fluorescent lighting, pristine leather chairs, granite tabletop. Mike arrived and sat at the end of the table.

"Well?" he asked the rhetorical question.

"You have our financials," Catherine looked Mike square in the eye.

"Not only that," Mike replied, "but your file was already pre-selected by the auditors for review. Not our auditors, these guys are federal.

"I have to hand it to you," he continued. "You gave it a go. But, it's out of my hands now. I know you want an extension, but the auditors will tell us how to classify your loan. There is not a lot of wiggle room."

"What happens next?" Jim asked.

"You can keep your planes, for now. You will get some demand letters from our attorneys. They sound really nasty, but don't take it personally, they're form letters. When the Feds finish their audit, you will get 20 days to cure the deficiencies. Then, you have to turn over the planes. So, I figure you can operate somewhere between 30-50 days from now."

Mike looked at Catherine. Jim looked at Catherine. "So, I got my extension," she smiled.

"Technically, we are foreclosing on the lease," Mike replied.

"But, I have 30 days, maybe more?" Catherine confirmed.

"For what it's worth," Mike nodded. "But, Catherine, I got a call from one of your board members yesterday, at your parent company. Technically, they guarantee the lease. I told him about our meeting today and he asked what was likely to happen with the auditors. He seemed nonchalant about the foreclosure, told me to proceed. It was an odd phone call."

"Which board member was it?" Catherine asked.

"Ripley, Al Ripley."

Lifeline

"Well, you got some time," Jim said, driving back to the Denver office. "But I wouldn't call it an extension."

"It's all the time I need," Catherine replied. "We may be out of covenant, but we are still a performing loan."

"But what is going to be different 30 days from now?"

"This." Catherine produced her phone and swiped over to voicemail. "This came in last night." She keyed in her password.

"Catherine, we have never met. My name is Kenneth Johnson. I am the CEO of Transpac. It seems like we had a little fun with your airline last week. I think we should talk. Give me a call."

"What's that all about," Jim was curious. "Does he want to call a truce on the fare wars?"

"The fare wars didn't exist," Catherine laughed. "The money we lost on those three flights was less than relocating aircraft after a big storm. And for Transpac, it wasn't even a blip in their budget."

"So, what does he want to talk about?"

"Same thing I want to talk about."

Gauntlet

When Catherine Nibali stepped off the plane in Dallas, it would be the last Outbound Air flight on the Denver-Dallas route. That was a fact. But the rest of the day was highly uncertain.

She was on time for her meeting with the board, but they were already seated when she entered the room. Catherine was like a condemned soldier cued up for the gauntlet. Al Ripley was in the room, but seated to the side of the giant table, lying in wait. Legal counsel was present. At the head of the table, sat Samuel Pierce, chairman of the board. No one made eye contact, except for Samuel. He had a job to do.

"I see our attorney is present," Catherine observed.

"Yes," Samuel nodded. "We thought that during our discussion, there might be a legal question that needed clarification."

"Good," Catherine replied. She pulled out a single set of papers, neatly stapled. "Then, perhaps our attorney can start with this."

"Ms. Nibali, there is no need to review your contract," Samuel leaned forward. "We all understand the termination provisions."

"That's not my contract," Catherine stared at Samuel.

"What is it?" he asked.

Doug MacBride stood up and walked over to Catherine. Across the table, he picked up the document in question. Scanning the cover sheet, Doug dropped it in front of the corporate attorney who was now the center of attention.

"Be careful, the ink is still wet on the signature page," Catherine warned.

"Well, what is it?" Samuel repeated.

The attorney quickly flipped from one page to the next. He looked up. "It's a codeshare agreement, between Outbound and Transpac. We are going to book our passengers on their flight legs. They are going to book their passengers on our flight legs. We will get a spiff on *our* passengers, and they will get a spiff on *their* passengers. From a customer perspective, it will look like we fly the major routes that Transpac flies. And it will look like Transpac flies on the regional routes that we fly. We will share the flight codes."

"I told you, she would pull something like this," Al Ripley exploded. "You have no authority to commit the future resources of Outbound to a binding agreement like this."

Agitation spread across the room, the din of sidebar conversations erupted. Catherine sat quietly. The attorney, absorbed in the codeshare document.

"Gentlemen, please," Samuel tried to restore order. "Ms. Nibali. I don't know that we are prepared to deal with this today. You should have provided us with some notice. We already made plans regarding the termination of your contract."

"Mr. Pierce. I was only able to secure this contract minutes before my flight down here this morning."

"What is this?" MacBride interrupted, standing over the shoulder of the attorney. "It says here that Outbound Air is prohibited from flying the Denver-Dallas route. You gave up our signature route for a period of five years. What else did you give up, Ms. Nibali?"

"Why, Mr. MacBride," Catherine responded. "You are talking to me like I am still the CEO of this airline. You fellows better make up your mind."

There was a sudden silence in the room.

"Alright then," she continued. "The Denver-Dallas route was a money loser, covered up in the numbers. Our planes are too small to fly that route competitively. Transpac has a dead operating cost about $85 a seat. When they blend their first class and business price points together, they can advertise their economy fare at $79 all day long. But our planes only have 70 seats.

Outbound's dead cost, one way is close to $145 a seat, without overhead. Our planes are too small to fly that route."

"So, what's this codeshare agreement all about?" Samuel asked.

"We have an agreement to team with Transpac. We will still fly out of Dallas and we will still fly out of Denver but to places where the market demand fits our aircraft. Part of the codeshare agreement requires Transpac to share their market data, so we can calculate our routes to fly full. If we fly full, we make money.

"Essentially, we re-deployed our aircraft from subsidized routes in underperforming markets to expanding routes in markets with proven growth. And we can make this happen quickly because we can codeshare through Transpac's reservation system."

"Well, I have some news for you, young lady," Al Ripley stood up. "I talked to your bank and they are about to foreclose on this little airline and take your planes away. So I don't know how you are going to codeshare when you don't have any aircraft."

"I anticipated that would be a topic for today," Catherine nodded as she reached for her cellphone. Two swipes across and a quick touch to speakerphone, she introduced Mike Hammermill to the group.

"Greetings, gentlemen," the voice from the small speaker filled the room. "I assume you are in your board meeting. Mr. Pierce. Mr. MacBride. Other members of the board. I understand Al Ripley is in the room as well. Mr. Ripley?" There was an awkward silence.

"Yes, Ripley, here."

"Good, Mr. Ripley. I took your call the other day for two reasons. Number one, your signature was on the original lease documents. Number two, you said you were a member of the board, representing the board."

Samuel Pierce looked at Doug MacBride. Doug MacBride looked at Al Ripley. Al Ripley stared at the floor.

"Now, Mr. Ripley, whether you are a board member or not," Mike continued, "I will leave your board to figure out. But, here is where we stand. Your lease agreements are currently under audit. However, I reviewed the codeshare agreement between Outbound and Transpac. Technically, that agreement does not put you back in covenant, but, I think we can see our way clear to monitor for another three months. The last thing we want to do is take those airplanes back."

Al Ripley continued to stare at the floor.

"Thank you, Mr. Hammermill," Catherine said.

"Gentlemen, if you have any other questions, Catherine can tell you how to reach me." The room was quiet. Catherine reached over to terminate the call.

Samuel Pierce was the next to speak. "Catherine. It seems you have another three months."

"Thank you, Mr. Pierce."

"So, Catherine, if you will excuse us. The board has some unfinished business with Mr. Ripley."

Transpac Flight to Denver

Jim greeted Catherine when she stepped off the Transpac plane in Denver. She shared the board's response. He shared the meeting between Javier's team and the Transpac team.

Jim drove home that night, in a good mood. During the past three years, he watched his airline pitch and roll, just out of his control. In a few short days, his earn-out period would be over.

He pulled into the garage and saw the sign. "Welcome home, Jim. You are about to begin the most important work of your day."

Postscript

At the end of his earn-out period, Jim Dunbar received only 57 percent of the agreement amount. The technical language of his contract prevented payments made from non-revenue miles on subsidized routes. Business is business and contracts are contracts. At the conclusion of the earn-out period, Jim was offered a position on the board of directors of Coriolis. He graciously accepted.

Catherine Nibali, over the next two years, brought Outbound into substantial profitability and expanded their flying routes by 30 percent. She would have continued to grow Outbound Air, but she took a position at Transpac as Vice-President of Operations. Seven years later, she took over as CEO.

One year after Catherine Nibali became CEO of Transpac, Fran Smith successfully negotiated the acquisition of Coriolis by Transpac. At the conclusion of the transaction, she left to start her own M&A firm.

Al Ripley was indicted for securities fraud based on insider trading at an unrelated company. He received a suspended sentence and is currently CEO of a mattress conglomerate.

Appendix

		Organizational Growth[vii]			
Level	Time Span Outlook	Organization Characteristics	Organizational Challenge	Management Challenge	Necessary Focus
VII	20-50y	International in scope, consisting of large scale value chains. This would include national government organizations, some private, but mostly public companies.	Structuring independent business unit portfolios around core long term objectives. Corporate governance, governmental regulation.	Finding executive talent with the capability to structure effective business unit portfolios, and the capability to establish and administrate corporate governance.	Identify and make markets, influence market trends for long term objectives. Identify long term social trends and build portfolios of business units effective in today's markets, able to adapt to next markets.
VI	10-20y	Portfolio company that leverages the capability of its individual business units to maximize profits in long term market cycles. Both private and public companies.	Cultural integration of acquired companies. Branding of individual products or services in a portfolio of independent business units. Government regulation.	Finding executive talent with the capability to identify and effectively work in conceptual market value chains.	Macro-markets and long term trends to leverage large scale markets on a national or emerging international scope. Attention to market perception and social stewardship.
V	5-10y	Legacy systems slow, organizational change and adaptation lags market demands.	Sustaining the machine, misplaced dependency on diminishing legacy sales.	Balance of internal operating systems with external market systems	Create a clear and compelling vision that remains relevant and nimble to a shifting market.
IV	2-5y	Expansion of branches, maturity of operating departments	Friction among operating departments, silos, alignment issues	Balance of systems for total throughput. Finding and training new managers.	Integration of systems and sub-systems into a whole system.
III	1-2y	Awareness of need to become profitable	Competition, costs, profitability	Efficiency	Create systems for efficiency and predictability
II	3-12m	Headcount increases, reactive behavior toward markets	Sales volume strains operational capacity, pursuit of more sales volume, difficulty for org to focus	Struggle to delegate while maintaining standards.	Define and document production methods and processes.
I	1d-3m	High risk of sustainability	Negative cash flow	Little or no management depth	Make sales, introduce product or service into the market

Properties in Levels of Work[viii]						
Level of Work	Longest Time Span Goals	Typical Managerial Role	Function	Tools	Problem Solving	Value
S – V	5-10y	Business Unit President, CEO	Creates relevant strategic vision in market	Financial models, market studies	External Analysis	Value in the marketplace
S – IV	2-5y	Executive Manager Vice-President	Integrates multiple systems and subsystems	System metrics	Systems Analysis	Multi-system efficiency, throughput
S – III	1-2y	Manager	Creates system Monitors system Improves system	Flowcharts, sequence, planning	Root cause analysis, comparative analysis	Single system efficiency, consistency, predictability
S – II	3-12m	Supervisor Project Manager Coordinator Project Engineer	Makes sure production gets done, implements the production system	Schedules, checklists, meetings	Experience, manuals, best practices	Accurate, complete, on-time
S – I	1d-3m	Production Technician Labor Clerical	Production	Real tools, equipment	Trial and Error	Quality

Additional Resources

The purpose of this story is to illustrate the fundamental elements of the research conducted by Dr. Elliott Jaques from 1950 until his passing on March 8, 2003. His findings constitute the science of everything we know about organizational structure.

We will continue to add resources and tools to this book at the following link – **www.outboundair.com**

You can learn more about the fundamentals of this research by subscribing at the following link – **www.timespan101.com**.

There are several organizations who continue to carry the message of Requisite Organization. The Requisite Organization International Institute is the copyright holder and publisher of the extensive library of books and learning materials created by Elliott Jaques. They can be reached at the following link - **http://www.requisite.org**.

The Global Organization Design Society maintains a list of practitioners and resources from around the world. They can be reached at the following link – **www.globalro.org**.

Dr. Stephen Clement worked directly with Elliott Jaques for several years at the Army War College and the CRA Mining Company in Australia. His most recent book, *It's About Work*, can be found at the following link – **www.organizational.com**.

Elliott's research continues to be carried out by a growing number of practitioners world-wide.

Levels of Work in the Behavioral Interview

The ideas contained in this story have compelling implications for the hiring process. A more complete discussion of levels of work and behavioral interviewing can be found at the following link – **www.hiringtalent.com**

Endnotes

[i] This model is adapted from a comparative study of two other models. First model is authored by Ichak Adizes, *Corporate Lifecycles*, 1988. Second model is authored by Elliott Jaques, *Requisite Organization*, Amended 2nd Edition, 1998.

[ii] This verse is adapted from a tune by James Cecil *Nurturing Customer Relationships*, a play on a song attributed to silver screen actress Mae West.

[iii] Elliott Jaques assumed that most team members come to work to do their best. He created this contract to codify that intention. Most discretionary decisions are related to the pace of work and the quality of output.

[iv] Work mode is a concept described by Wilfred Bion, *Experiences in Groups*, Tavistock Publications, 1961. Specifically defined as Basic Assumption Mental State, or BAMS. BAMS describes the mental state of a group in work mode or not in work mode. Brilliantly explained by Pat Murray.

[v] Renaming the meeting to the *President's Meeting* was the result of an agreement between Elliott Jaques and Wilfred Brown at the Glacier Metals Company in London, England, separately documented in *Exploration in Management*, Wilfred Brown, 1960 and *The Changing Culture of a Factory*, Elliott Jaques, 1951.

[vi] Level of work is adapted from the Requisite Organization model authored by Elliott Jaques, *Requisite Organization*, Amended 2nd Edition, 1998.

[vii] This is the appendix version of an organizational model adapted from a comparative study of two other models. First model is authored by Ichak Adizes, *Corporate Lifecycles*, 1988. Second model is authored by Elliott Jaques, *Requisite Organization*, Amended 2nd Edition, 1998.

[viii] This is the appendix version of level of work, adapted from the Requisite Organization model authored by Elliott Jaques, *Requisite Organization*, Amended 2nd Edition, 1998.

41810886R00131

Made in the USA
Charleston, SC
08 May 2015